"Nasar Meer weaves togethe
drawing on research in a nur
to address the question of
failure to achieve the objec
masterful account should become an important part of
future conversations by researchers and policymakers
about how we can lay the foundations for radical
change in this vital area of the social world."
John Solomos, University of Warwick

"Nasar Meer asks a thought-provoking foundational
question: What if racial justice movements are destined
to fail because racial injustice is part of the DNA of our
social institutions? He argues convincingly that only by
looking at these deep roots will we understand why racial
injustices prevail even after generations of anti-racism
struggles.... His deeply scholarly yet based-in-practice
account is a compelling wake-up call to rethink what
'progress' actually looks like and whose interests it serves."
Peggy Levitt, Wellesley College

"Timely and insightful, provides not only a clear
mapping of our current context with regard to racial
justice, what has been achieved, what has been obscured
and what has failed, but also what can be done. An
essential read in the current reactionary conjuncture and
provides us with ways in which to think about our past,
present and future in more hopeful and just terms."
Aurelien Mondon, University of Bath

"Asks profound questions about how struggles for racial
justice come to reach their impasse through counter-reactions
designed to preserve existing racial orders and formations.
Meer's book not only offers an illuminating analysis of the
present conjuncture, but also the challenge of thinking
through the concepts of racial justice and equality."
**Sindre Bangstad, KIFO, Institute for Church,
Religion and Worldview Research, Norway**

"A crucial analysis of what we can learn from various attempts at racial justice throughout the Global North. An accomplished scholar of race, ethnicity and nationalism, Meer's thorough and beautifully crafted text provides a needed guide for making sense of our present moment – and its historical antecedents – as both the Black Lives Matter movement and the global pandemic intensify."
Jean Beaman, University of California, Santa Barbara

"Nasar Meer enjoins us to reckon with the systemic character of racial injustice, the imprint of the past on the present and our compulsion to optimism in the face of the repeated failure of ameliorative initiatives. Alive to the moral, affective and political dimensions of its subject, this is essential reading for anyone who wants to understand the conditions which produce racial injustice and to imagine those which will allow the justified perseverance of hope."
David Feldman, Birkbeck, University of London

"Essential reading for anyone seeking a deeper understanding of structural racism and how it persists, despite waves of policy and political intervention."
Carol Young, Coalition for Race Equality and Rights

"For those scholar activists, community organisers, freedom dreamers and everyday people living the political and emotional struggle against racial injustice, this is a book for you. Meer offers a sobering reflection on how reckoning with what has not yet come to pass can in fact provide a renewed sense of hope in what might be."
Kennetta Hammond-Perry, Stephen Lawrence Research Centre, De Montfort University

THE CRUEL OPTIMISM OF RACIAL JUSTICE

Nasar Meer

First published in Great Britain in 2022 by

Policy Press, an imprint of
Bristol University Press
University of Bristol
1-9 Old Park Hill
Bristol
BS2 8BB
UK
t: +44 (0)117 954 5940
e: bup-info@bristol.ac.uk

Details of international sales and distribution partners are available at
policy.bristoluniversitypress.co.uk

For Aiisha Smith-Meer

What are the 21st century challenges shaping our lives today and in the future? At this time of social, political, economic and cultural disruption, this exciting series, published in association with the British Sociological Association, brings pressing public issues to the general reader, scholars and students. It offers standpoints to shape public conversations and a powerful platform for both scholarly and public debate, proposing better ways of understanding, and living in, our world.

Series Editors: Les Back, Goldsmiths and Nasar Meer, University of Edinburgh

Other titles in this series:
Published
Race, Taste, Class and Cars by Yunis Alam
Miseducation by Diane Reay
Snobbery by David Morgan
Money by Mary Mellor
Making Sense of Brexit by Victor Seidler
What's Wrong with Work? by Lynne Pettinger

Contents

About the author

Nasar Meer is Professor of Sociology and Director of RACE. ED at the University of Edinburgh, and was a Commissioner on the Royal Society of Edinburgh's (RSE) (2020–21) Post-COVID-19 Futures Inquiry, and a Member of the Scottish Government COVID-19 and Ethnicity Expert Reference Group. He is Co-Editor of the journal *Identities: Global Studies in Culture and Power*, and his publications include: *Whiteness and Nationalism* (ed, 2020); *The Impact Agenda: Challenges and Controversies* (co-authored, 2020); *Islam and Modernity* (4 volumes) (ed, 2017); *Citizenship, Identity and the Politics of Multiculturalism* (2015, 2nd edn); *Key Concepts in Race and Ethnicity* (2014); *Interculturalism and Multiculturalism* (ed, 2016), *Racialization and Religion* (ed, 2014) and *European Multiculturalism(s)* (ed, 2012). He is presently Co-Investigator on 'The impacts of the pandemic on ethnic and racialised groups in the UK' (UKRI, 2021–23) and Principal Investigator of GLIMER – Governance and Local Integration of Migrants and Europe's Refugees (JPI ERA Net/Horizon, 2017–21). He is an elected Fellow of the UK Academy of Social Sciences (FAcSS) and a Fellow of the Royal Society of Edinburgh (FRSE).

Acknowledgements

Much of the underlying research for this book draws on funded support from the Royal Society of Edinburgh (RSE), JPI Urban Europe and the Economic and Social Research Council (ESRC). I am immensely grateful for what such publicly funded research allows, and I remain indebted to my colleagues and collaborators for the continuing dialogues this has permitted. The teams at GLIMER, RACE.ED and *Identities* have been a constant source of community, care and intellectual vitality. Particular thanks to Katucha Bento, Michaelagh Broadbent, Ashlee Christoffersen, Gwenetta Curry, Tommy Curry, Agomoni Ganguli-Mitra, Radhika Govinda, Emma Hill, Sarah Hill, Gëzim Krasniqi, Mini Kurian, rashne limki, Kaveri Qureshi, Tim Peace, Shaira Vadasaria, Aaron Winter and Sophia Woodman. The reach of the 'Bristol School' is long and I continue to be grateful to Tariq Modood, Varun Uberoi and other members, as well as Claire Alexander, Christina Boswell, Nick Ellison, Linda McKie and Fiona McKay, for their support and mentorship in different guises over the years. Sincere thanks are due to my series co-editor Les Back, Victoria Pittman, Jo Morton, the manuscript reviewers and the entire publishing team, who have been typically motivating throughout the review process. The substantive parts of this book were drafted in the late evenings and early mornings either side of home-schooling. It was perhaps inevitable that my partner was writing a book in a similar fashion at the same time. It is hard to describe the bewildering intellect, strength and joy that is Katherine Smith, and so I will just say thank you. Finally, this book is dedicated to our daughter and intended as a solemn promise not to let work steal further time from her during these tender years.

ONE

The cruel optimism of racial justice

This book considers a seemingly simple question: what can we learn from success and failure in the pursuit of racial justice in the UK and elsewhere in the Global North? It is a question posed in the midst of ongoing conversations about possible turning points for racism and antiracism.[1] Globally, the Black Lives Matter (BLM) movement has grown in voice and dovetailed with undeniable racial disparities brought to the fore by the COVID-19 pandemic, and the response (or nonresponse) from governments to the underlying inequalities these have amplified. At the same time, and despite the departure of President Trump, this book charts how White nationalist movements have been elected to government in an increasing number of liberal democracies, and in ways that have made a virtue of racial injustice. The extent to which each of these developments is novel or reflects underlying tendencies is, of course, key, for how we understand them helps to determine how we try to respond. As such, the book's central question encourages us to grasp that while the specific events of our time may be distinctive, they necessarily reflect 'a past which in some sense is still living in the present'.[2]

This framing is necessary because the pursuit of racial justice in our present moment cannot be understood without reflecting on successes and defeats accrued over time. My argument is that there is no likely end to the struggle for racial justice, only the promise this heralds and the desire to persevere, even despite knowledge of likely failure. That is the cruel optimism of racial justice, and whose accumulated struggle invites us to recognise certain starting points. For any honest account of this topic must grasp that racial *injustice* is an intrinsic feature of societies in the Global North, something that is quickly apparent in at least two ways. Firstly, European nation-states, in particular, have seldom recognised their very formation through imperial systems built on racism, let alone their contemporary social, political or economic legacies. Secondly, the 'repetition without change'[3] that is engendered by the first concern, does not mean that racism is static. On the contrary, racism in Europe is routinely remade and redirected towards contemporary minorities. Among these are the very communities who, after the Second World War, helped to rebuild the societies that the bodies of their forebears first made wealthy. These are important starting points for, while 'racial justice is one of those terms widely used in everyday discourse, with a seemingly transparent reference',[4] a contention of this book is that we must give the idea of racial justice real world content by focusing on how, in and against these historical contexts, racial minorities have continued to mobilise for racial justice, and have done so while refusing the status of beleaguered objects of oppression.

The book therefore takes up Charles Mills' invitation to examine racial justice outside the realm of ideal theory,[5] an invitation that Mills crafted through a sustained critical engagement with the work in particular of the political philosopher John Rawls and his landmark text, *A Theory of Justice*.[6] The challenge Mills distils is to overcome the 'intellectual chasm' between a 'struggle for justice' and intellectual 'discussions of justice'.[7] Where this book diverges from Mills is in the definition of racial justice, which in his work means 'primarily not pre-emptive measures to prevent racial injustice but corrective measures to rectify injustices *that have already occurred*'.[8] Our discussion of racial justice is neither anchored in a debate with Rawls nor focused on corrective measures only. Racial justice is in contrast multi-temporal, as already indicated, in traversing that which has happened in the past, that which is manifest in the present, as well as that which will likely occur in the future. What the discussion nonetheless takes from Mills is the insistence that there is a rich and necessarily empirical story of racial justice that should be front and centre in discussions on this topic. In this respect, what follows is neither a celebratory nor pessimistic book. What is being argued is somewhat different: namely, that a prevailing, and perhaps dominant, view of racial justice in Britain has long been tethered to a 'cruel optimism'.[9]

This organising idea, of course, borrows from Laurent Berlant's influential account of the cultural logic at work in an increasingly unachievable post-war promise of the good life: a compelling and complex analysis that she develops with reference to art history, trauma theory and political studies. 'Optimism' in her argument is not the same as naivety or being 'co-opted' by state-agencies, and such like, but describes a sincere and, indeed, knowing attempt to 'repair ... what may be constitutively broken'.[10] As we discuss through the work of Hartman in particular,[11] by definition, racial justice stood outside the promise of the good life that occupies Berlant's account. For Afro-pessimist thought in particular, the challenge of racial justice exceeds prevailing humanist approaches, for these are ontologically anchored in an anti-Blackness, where the very category of 'human' is 'made legible through the irreconcilable distinction between humans and blackness'.[12] To understand the mobilisations for racial justice, and following Mills,[13] this book stands adjacent to this conceptual antagonism, neither captured by it nor entirely free from it, to argue that, while not readily speaking to racial justice per se, Berlant's motif is abundantly applicable to our topic, and through it we can encounter a novel means to understand the fate of racial justice today. This is to be found in the very real and necessary belief in the possibility of changing what is constitutively broken, and the work that our investment in this belief encourages, something captured in James Baldwin's comment: 'not everything that is faced can be changed, but nothing can be changed until it is faced'.[14] Many would recognise something in Berlant's description that:

> Optimism is cruel when the object/scene that ignites a sense of possibility actually makes it impossible to attain the expansive transformation for which a person or a people risks striving; and, doubly, it is cruel insofar as the very pleasures of being inside a relation have become sustaining regardless of the content of the relation ...[15]

It is the affective move in Berlant's account that resonates so centrally in the mobilisations for racial justice, in embodied responses to how something so morally unjust sits comfortably as normalised social outcomes, despite successive governments wielding the means to address it. This is at heart the question that motivates researchers, activists and minoritised groups who continually identify the drivers of racial inequalities, and who are long accustomed with the obfuscation that stymies change. 'The compulsion to repeat optimism', Berlant reminds us, 'is a condition of possibility that also risks having to survive, once again, disappointment.'[16] Berlant's notion of cruel optimism therefore deployed here offers something of bridge between affective experiences and social systems, or the relationship between feelings and governance.

Thinking in these terms can be understood as part of a wider interest in a 'new political economy of affects',[17] which variously theorises the political role of emotions in 'challenging, interrupting, and reconfiguring the predominant order',[18] and does so in ways that can 'bring to light how (and whose) affects and emotions are politically excluded, and how emotions are employed as a powerful line of demarcation'.[19] 'Emotions' in this meaning are not reducible to individual psychology but, rather, operate, in Ahmed's[20] terms, 'in concrete and particular ways, to mediate the relationship between the psychic and the social, and between the individual and collective'. Without this focus, it is hard to describe what motivates the pursuit of racial justice as something that is felt and embodied by racial *minorities* or, indeed, how racial *majorities* have felt able to enact racial injustices within prevailing systems. Among others, the sociologist W.E.B. Du Bois recognised this when he tried in his early work to bring together the affective trauma of racism within social systems in his discussion of double consciousness.[21] This included possibilities for transformation in his insistence that racial injustice creates 'a second sight',[22] a way of seeing things that escapes the notice of the majority, specifically the distance between democratic ideals and the practice of racial exclusion. As a consequence, 'once in a while', he described of Black Americans, 'through all of us there flashes some clairvoyance, some clear idea of what America really is. We who

4

are dark can see America in a way that Americans cannot'.[23] Then, much as now, these experiences are realised in everyday scenarios where responding to racial injustice begins by probing the deeper meanings and contradictions that give rise to a racialised experience.

This is why for Berlant's concept to work in the study of racial justice, especially with respect to *possibilities* becoming *impossibilities*, requires us to connect the idea of cruel optimism to the role of social systems and the function of racial projects. The proceeding discussion does this specifically to address an issue not central to Berlant's original thesis, but which thereby allows us to understand the relationships between our motivations and the impediments to racial justice across a range of arenas. Our discussion leads from remaking common membership, not least in nation-states (Chapter Two), and the optimism motivating attempts to tackle racism through public policy and institutional reform (Chapter Three), to their failures so cruelly illustrated in entrenched racial disproportionalities, exacerbated in the COVID-19 pandemic where physiological risks are routinely uncoupled from their systemic exposures (Chapter Four), and in models of governance for refuge and the cities of hope that might refuse the racialising misery of existing national asylum and refugee measures (Chapter Five), and on to the global White supremacy that underwrites so much of our present malaise more broadly (Chapter Six). Having traversed this, we can in the concluding chapter consider what this tells us about the ethics of social relations in our pursuit of racial justice (Chapter Seven). In so doing, the arguments in the chapters that follow will join and expand a presently US-centred critique of the idea of 'progress' in racial justice as something that relies on a 'teleological bent, presuming that society is ameliorative—gradually moving toward perfection—through incremental reforms or social action'.[24]

The argument in this book contends that such a view of progress ultimately rests in 'optimism's double bind', to quote Berlant, in which 'an image of a better good life available' creates an impasse that does not easily allow us to 'detach from what is already not working'.[25] One biographical narration of this dilemma is found in Leroy Logan's (2020) reflections on his

5

years in the Metropolitan Police force, a portion of which is dramatised in Steve McQueen's 2020 film *Red, White and Blue* as part of his widely acclaimed Small Axe series. Giving up a successful forensic science career to join the Metropolitan Police in 1983, Logan[26] was optimistic but never naive in believing that as a Black Londoner he could help change a racist institution from within, 'even though I knew that joining would set two worlds ... on a collision course'. For researchers, activists and policy makers committed to the pursuit of racial justice, there is something in this of the need to reckon with what we have long borne witness to, and often made a difficult peace with, which comes not in a single event or episode that typically characterises a trauma, but which is something more akin to an undulating pain and discomfort.

Some readers will recognise in themselves how we have routinely arrived at this impasse, and have perhaps even clung, in different ways, to the cruel optimism that racism in our societies can lessen, because some attitudes are less self-evidently hostile, signalling that systemic racial injustices might wither through concerted action over time. For my part, at least, it has led me to commit personal and family time to the roles that I felt might make a difference.[27] This should not be read as an admission of naivety or misplaced faith in the hope for change, or of having been 'hostage to the belief that everything is going to improve or turn out well'.[28] As Hague[29] has put it, 'one has to have an incredibly impoverished sense of political efficacy if one fails to see that "speaking truth to power" is not just one action but a whole strategic field that requires knowing when and how to do so'. As we encounter in Chapter Three, the cruel optimism of racial justice is necessarily dispersed across this field and in a constant struggle for something better, something possible, perhaps most keenly expressed in Neville Lawrence's statement to the Macpherson Inquiry (1999) into the racist murder of his 17-year-old son, Stephen Lawrence. 'We have to look forward', he insisted, speaking through grief. 'This is a very small place, this world of ours, we have to live together and we now have to say; let us put the past behind us, join hands and go forward.'[30]

These words, spoken by a parent surviving bereavement, appeal to the possibility that grief 'furnishes a sense of political community of a complex order, and it does this first of all by bringing to the fore the relational ties that have implications for theorizing fundamental dependency and ethical responsibility'.[31] *These words* remain a profound call for a better society, one greater than that which so cruelly took his son, but which, some twenty years later, remain unheeded. *These words* remind us how the past then, as the past now, is as ahead of us as much as it is behind us. For, in the findings of her inquiry into racial inequality and the COVID-19 pandemic, where 'Black, Asian and minority ethnic people have been overexposed, underprotected, stigmatised', Stephen's mother Baroness Doreen Lawrence issued another call to 'break that clear and tragic pattern'.[32] As discussed in Chapter Four, her report documented that 'the impact of COVID-19 is not random, but foreseeable and inevitable – the consequence of decades of structural injustice, inequality and discrimination that blights our society'.[33]

The continual attempt to pivot from a perpetual crisis to a turning point, as Baroness Lawrence has stressed, perhaps demonstrates how the greatest cruelty is that the embodied hope for racial justice remains; the desire to engage and try to change systems is one that endures, despite frequent and sobering evidence of some already entrenched racial inequalities deepening even further (as Chapter Three documents in detail). To further ground this for a moment, we might observe how in Britain one of the key points found in the 2020 Joint Committee on Human Rights report *Black People, Racism and Human Rights*[34] was not only that racial progress is far from advancing, but also that some things are demonstrably getting worse. Take the finding that 'in the last decade, the extent to which black children and young people are disproportionately targeted by the youth justice system has increased'.[35] This claim is easily substantiated by consulting youth justice statistics for 2018/19 in England and Wales, which show that Black children (who make up about 4 per cent of the entire population aged between 10–17 years) are four times more likely to be arrested than their White counterparts, and nearly three times more likely to receive a caution or custodial sentence. In 2019 the percentage of Black children in custody had significantly increased to 28 per cent of the entire population held in youth custody (compared with 15 per cent a decade previously).[36] As Chapters Three and Four detail, this is one among very many racially disproportionate outcomes that have worsened in real time despite at least eight other parliamentary publications since 2009, each of which made recommendations for addressing racial inequalities in Britain.

Relatively few such recommendations have been adopted, and indeed in its reply to the Joint Committee on Human Rights report, the present UK government refuses even to recognise the nature of the problem. For example, in response to the evidence of low confidence in policing among Black groups, the UK government has characterised this as reflecting not the lived experience of Black groups, but instead 'other factors outside their [the police's] control including media reporting, historical bias and use of statistics, which also have a significant effect on how people perceive policing'.[37] Clinging, then, to the hope of substantive governmental leadership is an example of something that 'actively impedes the aim that brought you to it initially'.[38] This sentiment is precisely what Dame Lawrence encourages us to move on from, something further empirically illustrated in a litany of other UK inquiry reports in recent years.[39] As will be shown in the proceeding chapters, what each of these reports makes plain is that in order to ignore that racial injustice is a key feature of disparities within and across these sectors, institutions and organisations must actively try to deny it.

This raises an important point that is infrequently considered by a number of researchers. In a recently published large-scale study finding significant discrimination against ethnic and racial minorities in the provision of public services, in a Nordic case with otherwise low levels of general inequality, researchers offer their evidence as 'important not just because it raises awareness of the problem to policymakers, but also because it can help solve the problem by holding a mirror to public officials, encouraging them to align their ideals and their actions'.[40] This begs the question, however: What if those ideals are already aligned to the existing racial injustices, because there is an acceptance that racial injustice is a necessary feature of social systems as they are presently configured? It is a basic question that has been straightforwardly answered by the Home Office, which recently confirmed it is aware of the likely indirect racial discrimination resulting from the Police, Crime, Sentencing and Courts Bill, and which it justified as follows: 'Any indirect difference on treatment on the grounds of race is anticipated to be potentially positive and objectively justified as a proportionate means of achieving our legitimate aim of reducing serious violence and preventing crime.'[41] The justification more broadly comes in light of the UK Government's Commission on Race and Ethnic Disparities (CRED), which makes a virtue of racial inequalities in presenting them 'as a beacon to the rest of Europe and the world'.[42] In what the Commission was persuaded is an uplifting account (as we return to in Chapter Three), their report seeks to pivot from the required focus on social systems, structures and institutions to – as we are told from the outset – 'the other reasons for minority success and failure, including those embedded in the cultures and attitudes of those minority communities themselves'.[43]

What Berlant's motif helps us to see, in this example and others, is that shocking racial equalities may appear traumatic when accounted for at one moment, but those of us in pursuit of racial justice have long adapted to 'a notion of systemic crisis or "crisis ordinariness"'.[44] Here (and as the COVID-19 disparities discussed in Chapter Four emphasise), '[t]he extraordinary always turns out to be an amplification of something in the works'.[45] In the pursuit of racial justice, however – and a key argument animating this book that we return to in each chapter – is that there are long-established tools in the study of racism that better allow us to take a 'systemic' approach when we discuss organisations, sectors, institutions and so forth. By broadening the aperture to observe the racialised nature of social and political systems that give rise to racial injustice we can explain how racial injustice can flourish without the need for choreographed and pre-meditated racist intentionality.

Cruel optimism and social systems

The initial idea for this book was to consider what possible futures might have been realised had available paths for racial justice been taken. While the final chapter does, indeed, consider how and what we can learn from the discussion in the preceding six, it quickly became apparent that a less utopian focus was required in order to set out how things might be done differently: namely, an account of why progress on racial justice has been so limited and failure so cyclical, and how racism prospers either in full sight or as an ever-present reality in our societies. Or, in other words, the ways in which the promise of racial equality exudes the cruel optimism of how 'something you desire is actually an obstacle to your flourishing'.[46] A good example is to be found in the opening statement of the Stephen Lawrence Inquiry, discussed in Chapter Three, in which the commissioners believed that 'such awareness of the problems directly and indirectly revealed' would herald 'a single opportunity to deal with specific matters arising from the murder and all that followed'.[47] As the proceeding chapters illustrate, it was an optimistic aspiration that cruelly rings hollow today. The questions for us are *both* how and why? The answer provided across the subsequent chapters rests in revisiting, and perhaps re-fashioning, an account of both 'social systems' and 'racial projects'.

Beginning with the first concern, Bonilla-Silva's profound account marked an important relocating of the study of racial injustice within the idiom of systems theory more broadly, specifically his description of 'a set of social relations and practices based on racial distinctions [that] develops at all societal levels'.[48] For our purposes, an 'idiom' here denotes a way of naming a series of social dynamics spanning agency and structure, and which share a family resemblance across different versions of systems thinking. As should be abundantly clear, therefore, the idea of social systems has a common concern amongst various iterations. As Klir once put it, '[a]lthough the name "system" may have different meanings under different circumstances and for different people, it ordinarily stands for an arrangement of certain components so interrelated as to form a whole'.[49]

The holism signalled here is not merely self-evident, but relies also on an underlying methodological emphasis. For example, one early proponent of this idiom, broadly conceived, was Von Bertalanffy, who anchored his idea of systems in the Aristotelian world-view that 'the whole is more than the sum of its parts', a seemingly simple statement that he maintained should be an organising principle of the 'system problem'.[50] Specifically, and leaning against the emphasis he saw in the 'second maxim' of Descartes' *Discourse on Method*, 'to break down every problem into as many separate simple elements as might be possible',[51] Von Bertalanffy and colleagues offered a somewhat more sociological idea of social systems than were popular in the social sciences, and especially mainstream sociology, in their day. Specifically, and attacking what prevailed in mainstream post-war functionalist thought, in particular, Von Bertalanffy pointed to an overemphasis on 'maintenance, equilibrium, adjustment, homeostasis, stable institutional structures, and so on, with the result that history, process, sociocultural change, inner-directed development, etc., are underplayed and, at most, appear as "deviants" with a negative value connotation'.[52] The prevailing approach to systems theory in the social sciences, he maintained, 'appears to be one of conservatism and conformism, defending the "system" … as is, conceptually neglecting and hence obstructing social change'.[53] In other words, *studying* social systems and *maintaining* them are self-evidently two very different things, and scholars explicitly invoking systems thinking in mainstream (White) social science at this time appeared more invested in the latter.

Conceiving of the social through the idiom of systems then has a long pedigree in the social sciences that can be pulled through in our present need to 'focus attention on specific features of the social order while recognizing that social processes are often multiply-determined'.[54] This is something neatly illustrated in Benjamin's rich study of the role of algorithms in social life. What she calls 'the New Jim Code' describes the ways in which contemporary 'tech designers encode judgements into technical systems, but claim that the racist results of their designs are entirely exterior to the encoding process. Racism thus becomes doubled, magnified and buried under new layers of digital denial'.[55] What this example so effectively illustrates is not only the interactions between systems and racial projects – an issue to which we return – but also how thinking in terms of social systems overcomes the 'boundary problem', including the 'effects of the state's activities [that] can be seen and felt in civil society without the actual presence of the state itself'.[56] What systems thinking traverses, however, is not only state–civil society boundaries, but a number of societal spheres that entrench and reproduce racial inequalities. These are precisely the ancillary spheres of systemic racial injustice that must be brought into view and understood as part of a whole.

Notwithstanding the 'Parsonian shadow of yesteryear', Hughey et al also appeal to the utility of systems, but specifically in what they describe as 'mechanisms'.[57] Borrowing from Hedström and Ylikoski,[58] they characterise these as 'a constellation of properties and actions of entities and activities that are organized to regularly bring about a particular type of outcome, and by which we may explain an observed outcome by referring to the precise and specific interactions that occur'.[59] This is a helpful way of thinking about regularity, process and outcomes independent of intentionality. In other work, something comparable is reflected in the idea of mechanisms, and specifically 'the mechanics of racialization',[60] and how this helps to link different social scales (of the micro, meso and macro), as well as bringing into focus how racialisation can serve as a hinge between agency and structure. In different ways, parts of this reading and that of Hughey et al[61] dovetail with the signature account of race and social systems advanced by Feagin,[62] a key feature of which he terms the 'white racial frame', and which he characterised as follows:

> Central to the persistence of systemic racism has been the development of a commonplace white racial frame—that is, an organized set of racialized ideas, stereotypes, emotions, and inclinations to discriminate ... the frame and associated discriminatory actions are consciously or unconsciously expressed in the routine operation of racist institutions ...[63]

What is especially appealing about this formulation is not only that it 'embodies' systems without requiring individual actions, but that it connects this embodiment to discursive practice, both of which are integral to an explanation of racial injustice. It is something which sets scholars concerned with race and social systems apart from scholars who emphasise the importance of ethnicity and cultural self-definition.[64] This is an important cleavage that is revisited in Chapter Two, and which in the present formulation tilts to a need to recognise how systems both sustain and are sustained by racial projects, and in turn rely on racial mechanisms that may share properties across different cases. For example, in writing from a US perspective, it is true that the history of Whiteness that Feagin views as underwriting the 'white racial frame' is specific to the case of *that* racial project, but as shown in Chapters Two and Six, it also offers generalisable properties in the racial mechanics that have globalised contemporary iterations of White supremacy. This includes an account of how a type of the White racial frame is not a peripheral to societies in the Global North, but often rests as an unstated core. In Chapter Six, this is discussed in terms of the social production of moral indifference[65] that it engenders, and which is manifest in many current projects of Whiteness that can, in turn, help to normalise and sustain White supremacy.[66] These may appear provocative statements, but they are also palpable matters that are empirically substantiated. The key concern at this stage is to grasp the linkages between racial projects and social systems, which Feagin and Elias help to facilitate in their description as follows:

> Systemic racism has routinely reproduced major societal institutions and networks that uphold asymmetrically structured material and social-psychological relations among racial groups. …
> In systemic racism theory, the past and present racial hierarchy and perpetuation of unequal socio-economic power relations among different racial groups are viewed as endemic to a race-based social system involving much more than conceptual meanings, ideologies and biased actions.[67]

These authors are keen to recognise their debt to past race scholarship, including, among others, W.E.B. Du Bois. Indeed, it is now more than a century since the publication of 'The Souls of White Folk', a short essay in Du Bois's *Darkwater*,[68] in which Du Bois brought together key strands from his earlier thought. 'The discovery of personal whiteness among the world's peoples is a very modern thing', he wrote, and one through which has been claimed 'the ownership of the earth forever', where 'the black world gets only the pittance that the white world throws it disdainfully'.[69] He continues:

> Everything great, good, efficient, fair, and honorable is 'white'; everything mean, bad, blundering, cheating, and dishonorable is 'yellow'; a bad taste is 'brown' and the devil is 'black.' The changes of this theme are continually rung in picture and story, in newspaper heading and moving-picture, in sermon and school book, until, of course, the King can do no wrong, – a White Man is always right and a Black Man has no rights which a white man is bound to respect.[70]

What Du Bois is describing here is how social and political hierarchies are symbolically and materially sustained through processes of signification, an argument that many years later has come to be characterised as forms of privilege. The role and function of Whiteness as privilege in contemporary literatures is discussed in Chapter Six, and Du Bois's account remains an immensely valuable historical record of theorising this not by focusing on individuals but on social and political processes, which seek to explain how and in what ways White racial self-interest refuses to yield its rewards. Returning to his absorbing account encourages us to think big: to traverse scales, questions of agency and structure, and matters of capital and community, and to be attuned to the ways in which Whiteness bears an expansive concept logic across different racial projects.

Cruel optimism and racial projects

'Attuned' does not mean limited to his time, however, for Du Bois's discussion resonates in the present *precisely* because its explanatory power has equipped other scholars with the means to understand the curation of past and present White supremacy.[71] Another way of describing curation in the race literature is to characterise it as a 'project'; something that comes into being in complicated ways, through often ambivalent processes of racialisation, and rarely through a singular agent's orchestration. As Chapter Two, in particular, will highlight, thinking in terms of racial projects allows us to consider this key question from Seamster and Ray:[72] 'How can racism be variable if racial hierarchy is enduring?' The answer presented in this book is to think of repeated racial mechanics that share racial logics, even as they operate in curating and sustaining different racial projects.

There are a variety of literatures that chart racial projects, namely, how 'racial projects link significations or representations of race, on the one hand, with social structural manifestations of racial hierarchy or dominance, on the other'.[73] This includes how the Irish, Italians and other immigrants to America (and, indeed, the Irish in Britain), became 'White' over time, and these provide well-established case studies in how the boundaries of Whiteness have functioned. For example, in his landmark study of Irish migration and settlement in the US, Ignatiev[74] sets out to examine how 'one group of people became white. Put another way, it [the book] asks how the Catholic Irish, an oppressed race in Ireland, became part of an oppressing race in America'. He continues:

> The Irish who emigrated to America in the eighteenth and nineteenth centuries were fleeing caste oppression and a system of landlordism that made the material conditions of the Irish peasant comparable to those of an American slave. They came to a society in which color was important in determining social position. It was not a pattern they were familiar with and they bore no responsibility for it; nevertheless, they adapted to it in short order.... To Irish laborers, to become white meant at first that they could sell themselves piecemeal instead of being sold for life, and later that they could compete for

jobs in all spheres instead of being confined to certain work; to Irish entrepreneurs, it meant that they could function outside of a segregated market. To both of these groups it meant that they were citizens of a democratic republic, with the right to elect and be elected, to be tried by a jury of their peers, to live wherever they could afford, and to spend, without racially imposed restrictions, whatever money they managed to acquire.[75]

A key implication here is that a focus on the social dynamics of racial projects, whether past or present, reiterates the ways in which processes of racialisation are not only 'state-led' but 'society-led'. This is to borrow from Palmer,[76] whose principal focus has been on the categories used to explain colonial and modern genocide. As discussed in Chapter Two, what is important here is the long shadow of how past constructs of Whiteness that were 'society-led', which would in practice rationalise 'to whom the state and its *associated* community considered itself to be responsible',[77] remain overlooked in the study of nations and nationalism in particular, and not least in how '"the nation" often stands as the mirror to which imperial identities are reflected back'.[78] What it also brings into view is the boundary problem between the state and civil society, which Mitchell,[79] among others, characterises as impossible to maintain, insofar as it becomes empirically very difficult to treat the goings-on in civil society as something which stands apart from the felt presence of the state itself. This is an issue returned to in the discussion of multi-scalar solidarities set out in Chapter Five, but what is important to note at this juncture is the tendency emerging across the accounts of Ignatiev, Palmer and Virdee, discussed further in what follows,[80] for a kind of paradoxical fragility in accounts of racial projects of Whiteness.

Centring the colonial genocide of Aboriginal communities in Queensland in the nineteenth century, and of Herero communities in South West Africa in the early twentieth century, Palmer documents in particular the fragility of Whiteness even in its genocidal dominance, where 'racial interbreeding and children of mixed parentage were thought dangerous to the dominant, "superior" white race'.[81] While not focusing on genocide, in his *Racism, Class and the Racialized Outsider,* Virdee[82] tracks a similar development in his discussion of how Britishness is reimagined and the racialised Irish become part of the working class. The role of the Whiteness in what we are calling a racial project is, for Virdee, how the inclusion of the Irish comes at the cost of consolidating another 'modality of racism' – namely antisemitism. Centring on political mobilisations around the Aliens Act 1905, Virdee[83] sheds light on how many socialist nationalists were complicit in a surge in antisemitism that informed the introduction of such racist legislation. Whether it was because 'Jews' were of an 'alien race' or the bearers of culture that they deemed was unassimilable, the socialist nationalists' refusal to integrate the Jewish worker into broader class struggles of the new unionism was a profound failing. As a consequence, Virdee continues:

> [D]emands for democratisation of the British political system were increasingly expressed, and, indeed legitimised in opposition to the 'non-white' African and Asian outwith its borders, just as they were already being legitimised in opposition to the Jewish enemy within. Through this racialised narrative of re-imagining, much of the British population came to know themselves fresh – as a white, Christian people.[84]

The challenge for Virdee instead is to develop a sociological concept of 'racialized outsider' – one that is theoretically transferable beyond the micro-encounter between different actors, and is especially able to incorporate social structure, but is historically meaningful and sensitive to resistance. Earlier on, we observed similar dynamics in Du Bois's notion of 'gifted second sight', an ontological perspective and sense of political clairvoyance, summed up by his statement that 'We in America can see America as it cannot see itself'.[85] The key point Du Bois was making is that projects of Whiteness are patterned by a variety of embodied hierarchies, and so it is only in being attentive to their social processes that we can render these visible. This is what is intended in the study of White privilege. Hence, 15 years after *Darkwater*, in his *Black Reconstruction*,[86] Du Bois elaborated an idea of White privilege as 'a sort of public and psychological wage', observed in a range of areas and principally turning on how White people are not socially sanctioned nor do they pay a political tariff for their racial status, while this 'seeming not to be anything in particular'.[87] Then, just as now, this is not purely a symbolic matter when 'from their ranks', as Du Bois observed, are drawn the police, the courts and the lawmakers. It would be impossible to summarise the broad influence of this body of thought, but an empirical account from the British case might be noted in Bhopal's study *White Privilege: The Myth of a Post-Racial Society*,[88] and more theoretically taken up in the burgeoning literatures on the political function of White ignorance discussed later. The affective character of Du Bois's concern, meanwhile, continues to resonate in contemporary accounts. This includes a recent exposition by Apata:

> On the whole, whites are free from the damaging effects of racism and bigotry, are unsaddled by the baggage of history and of constantly having to negotiate the tortuous and winding contours of daily discriminatory practices. They are not weighed down by the ever-present consciousness of the burden of a suspicious gaze heavy upon their shoulders, unworried by the dense foggy air of prejudice and stereotype that attends the lives of black people. They remain oblivious to the fact that their many privileges are made possible by the grinding suffocation of others, believing that everyone breathes the same clean air of freedom and privilege.[89]

Not knowing these experiences, and perhaps seeking not to know, has been characterised as a White epistemology of ignorance, and is sustained precisely against what Mills described as 'the dangers of an illuminating blackness or redness, protecting those who for "racial" reasons have needed not to know'.[90] The overarching discussion in the subsequent chapters of this book is also provoked by these concerns to reflect on how the spectacle of White supremacy also *relies on* White privilege, in the way the latter helps cultivate a social production of moral indifference which can facilitate the former.[91] This is not straightforward, but this book shows why it is an error to adopt an overly formalistic position to deny this in a way that negates the linkages. One example is the suggestion that we can only describe systems of racism but cannot attribute any agency to individuals that benefit from and preserve such systems. As Ray puts it, our focus should not be on 'exonerating actors', but instead on offering an account of systems that can help to explain 'divergent outcomes as the result of agency exercised in relation to organizational resources'.[92] The challenge here is to calibrate accurately the focus of inquiry to overcome, as Brown describes, a reduction of systemic issues to interpersonal ones, where:

> Power disappears as individuals are treated as the agents of the conflict and attitude is treated as its source. The prejudiced individual becomes the cause of and the tolerant one becomes the solution to a variety of social, economic, and political ills.[93]

Thinking then in terms of social systems also brings us into conversation with traditions of thought previously established in Critical Race Theory (CRT). Without wishing to rehearse a wide-ranging literature, a book such as this cannot overlook how questions of racial justice and injustice are the cornerstones of CRT, and so we turn next to some exemplary authors. As will become apparent, however, while the influence of CRT scholarship moves through my thought as much as that of any other person seriously committed to a deep and systemic analysis, this book does productively differ from it, not least in wanting to reflect on the need to understand the relationships between racial projects and social systems, something which helps to explain the embodied institutionalisation of racial injustice signalled earlier, without collapsing one into the other. This should not, however, be read as a disavowal of necessary intellectual chains; on the contrary, the purpose is instead to read theories in ways that try to take on board the intentionality of their authors.

Cruel optimism and surface flexibility

The desire not to attribute content to conceptual approaches concerned with deep-seated racial inequalities seems especially relevant to a tradition of thought subject to orchestrated and legislative opposition in a number of countries. Recently described as an 'extreme political stance'[94] by the UK government, CRT has its provenance in American legal discourse, and 'a counter-legal scholarship to the positivist and liberal legal discourse of civil rights'.[95] The focus within CRT has centred on the position of African Americans, and so emerged out of a focus on the historical, political and socioeconomic position of African Americans relative to White American society. Relationality to projects of Whiteness, therefore, has always been central to CRT approaches, and specifically how this relationship is contoured, if not determined, by questions of power. This is not intended as a benign description. The centrepiece of CRT approaches is that 'racism is normal, not aberrant, in American society'.[96] The 'normalisation' here, in Delgado's classic text *Critical Race Theory: The Cutting Edge*,[97] casts racism as having formed 'an ingrained feature of our landscape, [where] it looks ordinary and natural to persons in the culture'. He continues:

> Formal equal opportunity rules and laws that insist on treating Blacks and whites (for example) alike, can thus remedy only the more extreme and shocking sorts of injustice ... Formal equality can do little about the business-as-usual forms of racism that people of color confront every day and that account for much misery, alienation, and despair.

Perhaps an under-recognised feature of this process is the notion of a wider social desensitisation to racism, possibly signalled in Delgado's description of racism as 'business as usual'. A connected set of social processes are arguably characterised by other authors in their discussion of 'everyday racism',[98] and the subjective negotiation of this, which are not easily credited in CRT approaches. What is also perhaps overlooked relates to how 'desensitisation' in turn increases the thresholds for what constitutes 'real' racism, and this explains how, as Ahmed describes, it becomes 'wilful even to name racism, as if to talk about divisions is what is divisive. Given that racism recedes from the social consciousness, it appears as if the ones who "bring it up" are bringing it into existence'.[99] This is possibly what Goldberg gestures to as the phenomenology of race disappearing 'into the seams of sociality, invisibly holding the social fabric together even as it tears apart',[100] but it is also central to Hall's[101] account of race as a discourse which helps to narrate respective (and sometimes diverging) racial projects. In Hall's terms, this is because race:

> [o]perates like a language, like a sliding signifier, that its signifiers reference not genetically established facts but the systems of meaning that have come to be fixed in the classifications of culture; and that those meanings have real effects not because of some truth that inheres in their scientific classification but because of the will to power and the regime of truth that are instituted in the shifting relations of discourse that such meanings establish with our concepts and ideas in the signifying.[102]

The account of race as a 'chameleonic'[103] discursive formation does not sit comfortably with the more normatively anchored focus in CRT scholarship, and there are gaps too in the CRT literature where more needs to be elaborated as to the ambivalent mechanics of racialisation.[104] Often the CRT literature works with a broad brush in typically centring on the ways racial justice is 'embraced in the American mainstream in terms that excluded radical and fundamental challenges to status quo institutional practices'.[105] This is understandable since CRT scholars do not have to work hard to elaborate how the US was founded in ways that relied on treating Black African slaves as property, and then formally emancipated African Americans as socially, politically and legally lesser than Whites.[106] What is, of course, undeniable in the present assault on CRT is precisely its concern with deep-seated systems and their social manifestations, characterised in the motivation to taper back expansive concepts of racialisation to individual acts of irrationality unsanctioned by longstanding and systemic forces.

In some respects, the attacks are not wholly novel, and different American CRT scholars have then been enmeshed in these debates for at least a generation, commencing as they do with the implications of these historical relationships, before advancing the more normative position that a failure to question and acknowledge the function of racism is synonymous with acting to maintain White supremacy.[107] Much of this critique turns on the conviction that both tangible and intangible forms of racism are the principal means through which Whiteness continues to be privileged. Feagin and Elias recognise the ways in which their theories of systemic racism build on critical Black social thought, and indeed they begin with CRT's 'racial realism' which allows them to question 'the alleged progress of race-based human rights and claims of substantial advances'.[108] This is especially important for thinking about surface-level change that is, in many respects, symptomatic of the motif of cruel optimism narrating this book, since:

> Important partial or surface-level changes are widely cited and often become a distraction from more ingrained structural oppressions and deepening inequalities that continue ... The character of many racial changes suggests the concept of "surface flexibility", flexibility on racial matters that white elites utilize in framing racial realities.[109]

The utility of surface flexibility is manifest in a number of cases discussed in the ensuing chapters, from political rhetoric to public policy and, indeed, law, and offers a 'mechanism' through which the cruel optimism of racial justice pervades. In contrast, by seeing racial injustice as conventional and not exceptional, drawn across social systems by racial projects, we would be better placed to grasp the nature of the problem we face. This is the key to understanding the cruel optimism of racial justice, because it foregrounds how policies promoting antiracism become focused on addressing unambiguous forms of racism, even while there is a parallel normalisation of what ought to be considered extreme. So, running alongside observations about desensitisation, CRT scholars have long been interested in the nature and function of so-called 'smokescreens', which continue to bear relevance.

As this chapter stated at the outset, however, this should not encourage a totalising approach that forecloses agency, minimises resistance, and collapses the refusal of racial minorities into mere objects of racist social systems. On the contrary, what is being worked towards in the idea of racial projects is that these systems have identities, and in the next chapter we will consider how and in what ways these have been made, in order that they re-made. The important point to reiterate, is that cruel optimism is not the same as defeat by the persistence of racialised historical projects that shape our present. The pursuit of antiracist sensibilities at the level of interpersonal and systemic practice speak to a continuing insistence for better social systems. In this regard, and while we may 'pray for the dead', we must continue to 'fight like hell for the living'.[110] As we return to in Chapter Seven, the challenge is as much ethical as it is procedural, in cultivating not only a 'shared fate', which 'comes by virtue of being entangled with others in such a way that one's future is tied to theirs',[111] but something akin to an antiracist humanism in which 'what is common to humans is not rationality but the ontological fact of mortality, not the capacity to reason but vulnerability to suffering'.[112]

These quite conceptual concerns are commonly anchored not only in theoretical literatures but also in the biographies of racial minorities, including that of myself and my siblings. For, as the children of Commonwealth citizens who laboured unskilled in declining industries, we had the essentials growing up but we were what I would later come to understand as 'asset poor'. Our parents did their very best and were rich in dignity, but the local state was our benefactor. After becoming familiar in later years with literatures discussed in this book, I came to understand the dynamics at work in everyday and normalised encounters that my parents would have with our local authority in West Yorkshire. Their English was poor and so one of us invariably went along to translate. What we routinely experienced was a system that had developed structures and institutions which racially stratified available services. As administrators, local welfare officers were themselves 'coping' but they did so through racialising and making access difficult, requiring minoritised clients to wait for services and withhold information, all intended to decrease demand and make their jobs more manageable, for example, my dad being asked to take a ticket to wait even though the reception knew they would not see him nor many of the other minoritised clients that day. My parents struggled against this, with the means they had, and principally an optimism that the system would do better for those that came after them. As my sister described many years later in a dedication to my father:

> A strong sense of social justice and civic duty ran deep in my father. He was a shop steward with the National Union of Dyers, Bleachers and Textile Workers for many years. A Labour Party stalwart, he was renowned as a formidable canvasser. He was also an advocate for others in the community and campaigned tirelessly on behalf of ethnic minority parents, setting up a Muslim parents' association which worked against racism in schools.[113]

What I and many others learned from pioneer generations was that racial justice would require systemic change and touch majorities as much as the minoritised. As such, my particular story is also connected to many others that cumulatively offer an empirically emergent account of racialised social systems. My 'personal troubles', as C. Wright Mills[114] so memorably put it (I would later come to learn), could not be solved merely as 'private troubles', nor should the resolve of racial minorities to devise a means for a better society be overlooked, something to which I hope this book does justice.

Chapter outline

To take up these concerns, in 'Reimagining nationhood?', Chapter Two will turn to the principal means through which racialised boundaries are presently enacted, specifically in how national identities are imagined. What are the ways in which these insider/outsider boundaries can be recalibrated so that they can also be traversed? This chapter will take the example of what is sometimes called Britain's multicultural moment, where at the turn of the millennium an opening to rethink the national story was presented in state-of-the-nation-type report by activists and scholars, which held the public conversation. Published by the Runnymede Trust in 2000, the *Commission on the Future of Multi-Ethnic Britain*,[115] to give its full title, is a salutary lesson, precisely because of its attempt to reconcile a changing national identity with an honest and necessary account of its origins; to narrate a country that did not disenfranchise its black and ethnic minorities. It was hoped that such an approach would at least begin to invalidate the social and political inequalities that manifest. How and why did this not come to pass, and what was lost in the maelstrom of opposition to it?

This is followed by a discussion on 'Equality, inequalities and institutional racism', where Chapter Three considers how we tackle processes of racialisation that are not self-evidently sustained by individual attitudes alone, and which are not formally sanctioned in public policy? This is what the issue of institutional racism focuses on, something that makes convention the key, and individual motives and objectives less relevant to the continuation of racialised outcomes. One word which relates to what is being described here is 'unwitting', and this is precisely how institutional racism came to be described in an inquiry into the London Metropolitan Police Service. This followed a long campaign by the parents of the teenager Stephen Lawrence, who was murdered by a group of White young men and whose death was improperly investigated. In the official inquiry undertaken by Sir William Macpherson, which came to be known as the Macpherson Inquiry, the investigating judge found the police service guilty of 'unwitting racism', deemed an outcome of institutional racism, and so made a number of wide-ranging recommendations with a broad scope which then had implications outside the police force in a manner that related to the public sector more broadly. Fast forward a quarter of a century, and what was achieved, partially and wholly, and what objectives did we fall short of, and why?

Picking this up in 'The racial realities of COVID-19', Chapter Four turns to the disproportionalities made so starkly visible by the pandemic, and dwells on why countries have been so reticent to consider how racism heightens vulnerability to COVID-19 at all levels of society (across deprived and high-income social groups). Certainly, health inequalities policies in different countries have looked at deprivation and socioeconomic inequalities,[116] but COVID-19 made it clear that race also needs to be a distinct focus, because 'intersections between socioeconomic status, ethnicity and racism intensify inequalities in health for ethnic groups'.[117] The key point is that, as Phelan and Link observe, 'if racism is a fundamental cause of health inequalities, then the fundamental cause must be addressed directly'.[118] The chapter will explore this as an ongoing issue, of course, and moving beyond the peaks of high infection it will show why it is essential that societies focus on the racial determinants of health, in ways that can improve social protection and social equity for all our communities. What does this require that is different from what has been pursued up to now?

Chapter Five, slightly pivoting to an adjacent focus in the pursuit of racial justice, will consider what we can learn from recent developments to ask if it is possible to de-racialise refuge. According to the International Organization for Migration (IOM), over 1.6 million displaced migrants and refugees entered Europe in 2015 at the height of the so-called refugee crisis.[119] By the middle of 2020, COVID-19 largely brought the movement of people to a halt as individual states and whole regional blocs introduced travel restrictions. Some have been more cautious than others in accounting for international laws and conventions intended to protect the right to entry for refugees and asylum seekers, but overall the picture is bleak.[120] In this chapter we will consider the emergent modes of governance that developed which especially relied on associations from the third sector which have assumed a key role in what Elia has termed 'bottom up welfare'.[121] To what extent can these local approaches begin to offset the racialised national discourse and policy, or at least reflect something of the ways in which racial formations are 'confronted and broken down'?[122]

In Chapter Six, the penultimate chapter 'Whiteness and the wreckage of racialisation', we will consider the decade since Anders Behring Breivik's murderous rampage in 2011 at a summer camp held by the youth wing of the Norwegian Labour Party. Breivik's main targets were those he called multiculturalists and cultural Marxists, gunned down for undermining his vision of a White Christian Europe. In all, 69 young people and children were killed on the island of Utøya, and a further 8 people perished in the associated bomb attacks in Oslo. This chapter will consider how in many respects these people were equally the victims of a lethal ideology that, as Mondon and Winter[123] have noted, has been normalised in mainstream politics, aided and abetted by commentators who draw from a common well. Brenton Tarrant, the Australian who gunned down 51 adults and children during Friday prayers at two mosques in Christchurch, chalked Breivik's name on his weapons and livestreamed his attack to many of Breivik's Facebook followers. Tarrant also made prominent on his weapons the insignia '14 Words' – referencing the White genocide motto propagated by David Lane (a neo-Nazi who died in a US prison in 2007): 'We must secure the existence of our people and a future for white children'. In Charlottesville, Virginia, this was rendered down to the slogan 'You will not replace us' which was chanted by White nationalist demonstrators following the election of the 45th President of the United States. The underlying belief for Breivik, Tarrant and others is that non-Whites, especially Muslims, are invaders, intent on replacing the White majority in Europe and the West more broadly though a numerical challenge, political subversion and cultural domination. Why have liberal democracies increasingly mainstreamed this White supremacy, and what might have been done in the wake of Utøya to counter it?

In the concluding chapter we will consider how we might learn from all that has proceeded, so that the future of racial justice escapes that cruel optimism that presently contains it. It is argued that this requires imagining a different *present* as well as future, one that can transform the cruel optimism of racial justice into a justified perseverance of hope.

TWO

Reimagining nationhood?

The objective of racial justice is greater than public policy per se, because it invites us to reflect on the character of our societies by asking who and what we think we are, and seek to be. Another way of putting this is to say that social systems carry identities too, and this chapter will argue that the public policies we enact to advance racial justice have been received in an 'idea of community ... connected with sets of political values'[1] that are already underwritten by identity claims. Grasping the historical features of these contingencies is imperative and goes beyond what Bevir and Rhodes[2] have termed the 'web of beliefs' in which certain policies should rest, such as the statutory requirements of race equality legislation discussed in Chapter Three. The public ambition is much greater than the enactment of policy alone. An immediate question, however, is: What helps to constitute 'ideas of community' that can be manifested in 'political values' and 'webs of beliefs'?

To answer this question, and thinking specifically about meta-membership in any given society in the Global North, there is presently no getting away from the centrality of the nation-state for, in the end, 'we have to put it somewhere'.[3] This is not to overlook a long and established set of critiques and normative preferences which offer cosmopolitan framings (broadly conceived), or more bottom-up ways in which antiracism may be pursued. When we embark in Chapter Five on the discussion of cities, solidarities and the idea of the 'multi-scalar', this national-level framing will in fact be directly challenged from the *bottom up*. From the *top down*, however, the meta-membership that social systems enact is not satisfactorily understood *purely* through a cosmopolitan or transnational framing alone. One way of insisting on this point is to follow Burton's question: 'Who can afford to be sanguine about (or oblivious to) needing the nation?'[4] For it is no accident that those groups who mobilise to reimagine nationhood are also those for whom exclusion from it comes with 'material dispossession and political disenfranchisement'.[5] While these are both present-centred and future-oriented concerns, it would be myopic to try and understand them apart from the larger historical pattern that constituted them. This is because nation-states, are part of a crucible of racial injustice well beyond their present iterations, and have imported much from an imperial mode that largely relied on race-making, in ways that variously sought to fashion the world in their interests: to claim 'the ownership of the earth forever', as Du Bois so memorably put it.[6] In this respect, argues Moses, the modern nation-state is not the simply a '"sovereign ontological subject" of explanation', for it must instead be explained through 'an account of European modernity that links nation-building, imperial competition and international and intra-national racial struggle to the ideologically driven catastrophes of the twentieth century'.[7] One of the implications of this framing is that interior and exterior racial injustices cannot be deemed 'aberrant offshoots'[8] from the *creation* and *curation* of nation-states, for to do so is to deny a 'reciprocity of determination'[9] between race-making and nation-making. This is partly why some have argued that the contemporary appeal to nationhood cannot break free of this relationship, and so is best understood through an equivalence with race, since 'ideas of 'race' and 'nation' are both categories of simultaneous inclusion and exclusion':

> Herein lies a process of reification because the criteria of inclusion/exclusion are made to appear as the determinants of groups' differentiation rather the act of signification, the reproduction of the act of signification, and the ordering of the material world in ways consistent with the act of signification.[10]

Among the issues that this view ignores, however, are the challenges, revisions and contestations of racial minorities, which seek to recognise racial histories in order to remake founding narratives, not least through the force of reimagined identities. To read nationhood as a flattening process of racialisation without taking seriously how racial minorities confound certain notions of hierarchy within it can only ever offer a partial view. It is precisely the form and content of nationhood, whether or not one holds cosmopolitan, transnational or antinational identities, that the pursuit of racial justice cannot vacate. This further demands we engage with a set of literatures on the idea of nations and national identities as well as the attempts to remake membership through these categories, not least in Britain, and particularly by racialised minorities themselves.

As such, this chapter will take the example of what is sometimes called Britain's multicultural moment where, at the turn of the millennium, an opening to rethink stories of Britishness was presented in a state-of-the-nation-type report by activists and scholars, which held the public conversation. Published by the Runnymede Trust in 2000, the Report of the Commission on the Future of Multi-Ethnic Britain[11] is a salutary lesson, precisely because of its attempt to reconcile a changing national identity with an honest and necessary account of its origins; to forge a narrative that did not disenfranchise its Black and ethnic minorities. It was hoped that such an approach would begin to invalidate the normality of the social and political inequalities encountered by racialised minorities, and perhaps even offer some scope to un-make certain features of a society 'structured in dominance'.[12] What was lost in the maelstrom of opposition to it are issues that we find instructive on revisiting. As Chapter Six shows, this is a crucial question precisely because a key means through which racialised boundaries are presently being drawn and redrawn, specifically in the Global North, rests in the ways national identities are being reimagined.

Unfinished conversations

In all of the proceeding talk of identities, it is worth emphasising there that we are working with dynamic categories. In this regard, as Bauman once argued, identities necessarily have 'the ontological status of a project and a postulate'. He continued: 'To say "postulated identity" is to say one word too many, as there is not nor can there be any other identity but a postulated one'.[13] This is not the same as saying that identities are a fiction. What it means, and as will be explored in the discussion of a dominant strand within nationalism studies, is that all identities are imagined and often amount to unfinished conversations, as we learn from Stuart Hall.[14] If we step back from its social science usage, we can note Hawthorne's description that identity, in its simplest sense, reflects the relationship 'that each thing has to itself and to nothing else'.[15] This he traces to ways of thinking about identity in mathematical forms, something that Calhoun broadens out when he situates the provenance of identity within 'a technical origin in philosophy, beginning from the ancient Greeks, as well as in mathematics and biology. Aristotle pursued identity in terms of the relationship between "essence" and "appearance", or between the true nature of phenomena and epiphenomenal variations'.[16] What is interesting is that even following its migration into the social sciences, identity did not assume in scholarly discourse the centrality it does today until relatively late on. This has changed partly because of a wider set of methodological developments in the social sciences, including the cultural turn and elevation of the subject. As Hall wrote, this reflected:

> the growing complexity of the modern world and the awareness that this inner core of the subject was not autonomous and self-sufficient, but was formed in relation to 'significant others', who mediated the subject values, meanings and symbols – the culture – of the world he/she inhabited. … Identity in this socio-logical conception, bridges the gap between the 'inside' and the 'outside' – between the personal and the public worlds. The fact that we project 'ourselves' into these cultural identities, at the same time internalizing their meanings and values, making them 'part of us', helps to align our subjective feelings with the objectives places we occupy in the social and cultural world.[17]

A critical and visible study of race has been central to developing this understanding, something that has not been universally welcomed. Amid the disquiet, some two decades ago, Brubaker and Cooper lamented the social sciences as being in thrall to identity, something they concluded has regressive outcomes:

> the social sciences and humanities have surrendered to the word 'identity'; that this has both intellectual and political costs … and tends to mean too much (when understood in a strong sense), too little (when understood in a weak), or nothing at all (because of its sheer ambiguity).[18]

Part of their complaint is that identity has become a ubiquitous explanation rather than something in need of explaining. In other words, in their view, the study of identity in the social sciences conflates categories of practice with categories of analysis. Key here is how the study of race and racism often emphasises the importance of group identities as a sociological resource as well as normative categories. As we return to in Chapter Three, one reason for this is most certainly not unique to race and concerns how group identities 'counteract inherited negative stereotypes, defend more positive self-images, and develop respect for members of their groups'.[19] This is partly the role we can observe racial identities playing in terms of self-definition. This does not mean to imply that minoritised racial groups have singular identities. As Young describes, 'as products of social relations, groups are fluid; they come into being and fade away'.[20] The point instead is to grasp how and in what ways 'group identity may become salient only under specific circumstances [since] most people in modern societies have multiple group identifications, moreover, and therefore groups themselves are not discrete unities'.[21]

The particular challenge that racial minorities encounter here is that in mobilising a form of racialised identity politics, group categories may risk restating rather than deconstructing the means to racialise in the first instance. This is what I've referred to as the 'paradox of race',[22] where, conversely, to say that race is a social construct does not deny that it has real social and economic consequences. If we therefore choose to ignore race in public policy, we also ignore how racial categories are embedded in the routine operations of social systems. So the paradox is that we need to recognise race to challenge racial injustice. This includes recognising how the vehicle for inclusion can sometimes invoke and repudiate the differences that have been denied inclusion in the first place. Perhaps this is equally true of other historically oppressed minorities who mobilise for justice using group labels first forged through (and later against) that oppression. Notwithstanding, the general observation does not fully resolve the tension but, as McCarthy has argued:

> [I]t makes little political sense to maintain that a group identification forged during centuries of brutal oppression could or should be dissolved while the injuries still persist. To proscribe race consciousness for remedial purposes without removing the racial inequities produced through racial classification for purposes of domination would be a fateful political error. Moreover, as the abolitionist and civil rights movements demonstrate, it is a vast oversimplification to claim that the race consciousness forged in struggles against racial oppression merely reinforces a consciousness of victimization. Indeed, depending on circumstances, such struggles may well enhance a group's sense of effective agency and transformative power.[23]

One route to overcoming the tension registered here is to differentiate between conceptualising people's identities and processes of identification. This allows us to understand how social and political processes help to forge identities, individual and group, which in turn forge social and political processes. To Sicakkan and Lithman, 'the term "identification" enables one to conceptualise identity both in terms of individuals' own choices of identity references and of other persons' identity attributions. That is, individuals can both identify with and be identified as "something".'[24] The important point here is that processes of identification are rarely straightforward reflections of personal choice but often comprise a response (sometimes a challenge) to prior systemic processes of categorisation outside the control of minoritised racial groups.

Nations, states and empires

Any focus on racial minority identities, therefore, cannot be asymmetrical, which makes it imperative that we focus also on how insider/outsider boundaries function (and can be reassembled) in nation-states. Across the pages of this book we can observe how these seemingly symbolic concerns have profound material outcomes. These include the ways modern nation-states have always tied racial symbols to criteria of citizenship. Typically seen as a compact between people and the state, a relationship that grants certain 'rights' (such as voting, legal protection and free education) as long as those deemed members adhere to certain 'duties' (for example, obey the law, pay taxes, even participate in jury service if asked), such ideal types of citizenship routinely overlook that membership of nation-states has from the outset been identity-based too, in ways 'pervading not only the "state" [but also the] "economy" and "civil society"'.[25] Rather than an afterthought, indeed, identity in nation-states has been the means through which access to a full spectrum of citizenship is routinely afforded, extended and, indeed, withdrawn.

As we revisit in Chapter Five, and as Agamben's discussion of modern sovereignty shows, part of the nation-state's 'inner contradiction' comes in the ways identity functions as a lynchpin of sovereignty. In his terms, 'the bearer of rights and ... can only be constituted as such through the repetition of the sovereign exception'.[26] What might these 'inner contradictions' resemble? As we encounter in the discussion of cities and governance, a present example is found in De Genova's description of the ways 'both labour migrants and refugees who cannot secure visas are compelled to first arrive on European territory as "unauthorized" asylum-seekers, and hence, as de facto "illegal migrants", who only thereafter may petition for asylum'.[27] In these cases, identity matters in politically disqualifying them as a member of the state, leaving them caught in what Agamben terms a 'zone of indistinction'.[28] In the case of those seeking refuge, in particular, and reduced to 'bare life' without a status that protects them, what is described here is apparent in how the European Union (EU) 'for the last two decades, has actively converted the Mediterranean into a mass grave'.[29]

Before turning, in later chapters, to Goldberg's insistence that nation-states are straightforwardly racial states,[30] in their organisation of citizenship, belonging and access to the polity more broadly, what we need to do here is to pay attention to three things: the ways in which national identities may be 'imagined' in nation-states to reflect or unsettle the alleged shared characteristics of its members; the ways this imagining purportedly differentiates its members from people in another nation-state; and the ways in which the formal identities of nation-states are not the same thing as people's national identities, the former being principally forged by *majorities* against *minorities* in nation-states.

The term 'imagined' here is used in the way that the historical sociologist Benedict Anderson set out in his book *Imagined Communities*,[31] a landmark account in the field of nationalism studies more broadly. Alongside other 'modernists', Anderson argued that nationalism emerged in Europe in the 18th century and *created* nations as 'imagined political communities' that are both 'limited and sovereign'.[32] By this he meant a number of things. Firstly, nations are imagined insofar as all members of even the smallest nation will never meet each other, and yet in the minds of each lives an image of their connection to each other, and so connects 'their horizons in the mind's eye'.[33] Secondly, nations are 'limited' because each nation has finite borders beyond which live other nations. Thirdly, nations are 'sovereign' because they were created in an age of modernity when the legitimacy of rule by monarchies was in decline. Lastly, he argued that, regardless of the actual inequality, the nation is always conceived as a deep and horizontal comradeship, but one which simultaneously passes over an often 'turbulent and contested history', specifically by giving emphasis to 'tradition and heritage, above all on continuity so that our present political culture is seen as the flowering of a long organic evolution'.[34]

There are two immediate implications here for our discussion: firstly, the need not to confuse the term 'imagining' with *fabrication* – just because people imagine their social and political order as a 'national' one does not mean it is not a 'real' basis for social and political organisation. Secondly, the role of 'turbulent histories' and alleged 'finite borders' is key, for in them we can find a resource for understanding racial injustices today, and possibly even the means to traverse the 'confounding distinction between inside and outside'.[35] Beginning with the first point, Anderson identifies the emergence of the printing press – giving rise to what he called 'print capitalism' – as something which did more than anything else to allow people to imagine themselves as a nation. In Europe, this facilitated the development of commercial book publishing on a mass scale precisely at a time when Latin was declining as the main European script. This meant that more regional languages – or 'vernaculars' – were ascendant and provided the basis for a national language. This was particularly evident in the circulation of newspapers simultaneously consumed by an increasing number of reading masses. The widespread availability of these and other texts in the same vernaculars allowed the reader to imagine much in common with their co-reader.

What such developments also heralded is the emergence of what Anderson called 'calendrical symmetry', insofar as they placed everybody in the country in the same time frame. It is a feature of the modernist account that is profoundly troubled when the question of race is brought into view, not least in what Hanchard has described as 'racial time'.[36] There are a number of facets to this wide-ranging account that punctures the notion of a unified temporal zone that is so key for Anderson and others. One is the 'ethico-political relationship between temporality and notions of human progress',[37] that is, the teleological view that European modernity has set the chronometer for progress, or, as Connell has also put it, the view that other social orders were overwhelmed 'not because Europeans with guns came and shattered them, but because modernity is irresistible'.[38] The omission of the former rationale in favour of the latter is a point we return to, but it is very powerfully stated in Mazower's characterisation of a 'widely-held unspoken assumption that the mass killing of African or American peoples was distant and in some senses an "inevitable" part of progress'.[39] Recognising the dynamics of racial time is also relevant for our discussion in other ways, including how racial time compels us to register 'the inequalities of temporality that result from power relations between racially dominant and sub-ordinate groups'.[40] Hanchard continues:

> Unequal relationships between dominant and subordinate groups produce unequal temporal access to institutions, goods, services, resources, power, and knowledge ...When coupled with the distinct temporal modalities that relations of dominance and subordination produce, racial time has operated as a structural effect upon the politics of racial difference. Its effects can be seen in the daily interactions—grand and quotidian—in multiracial societies.[41]

Racial time takes on a particularly present and acute illustration in Chapter Four where, in effect, it helps to explain who lives and who dies during the COVID-19 pandemic or, more precisely, how a system synchronised according to racial time underscores the disproportionalities so manifestly apparent. The rationale motivating these arguments is not only present-centred, of course, for it is also moved by a desire to improve the prevailing historical understanding in which race is minimised as part of a 'narrative contract'[42] between the nation-states and their narrators. Doing something different in this regard requires 'unmasking the complicity of history-writing in patrolling the borders of national identity as well'.[43]

It is notable how relatively few of the canonical European scholars in the field of nations and nationalism had much to say, for example, on the role of Empire and, with the exception of Anderson, virtually nothing to say on racism in the formation of nation-states. In comparable ways, it is fair to say these authors viewed European imperialism as incidental to European nation-state formation, insofar as 'the core or essence of nationalism' had allegedly long since been 'laid out'.[44] This is not to say that such authors thought nationalism inevitable, much more that race was inconsequential. Given the entanglement of European modernity (for Gellner and other 'modernists', the seed-bed of nations and nationalism) in Empire, this seems odd to say the least, and is reminiscent of J.R. Seeley's remark that the British Empire was acquired in 'a fit of absence of mind'.[45] That such oversights were formative to an area of study is perhaps one reason why nationalism studies and race scholarship have largely proceeded in parallel, even while the latter has taken a deep and substantive interest in historical and archival narrations of the nation-state. Hartman draws out the implications of such oversights in her study of the afterlife of slavery, something that should not, in her terms, be seen as 'an antiquarian obsession with bygone days or the burden of a too-long memory'. On the contrary, across nation-states in the Global North it is manifest in the ways that 'black lives are still imperilled and devalued by a racial calculus and a political arithmetic that were entrenched centuries ago'.[46] She continues:

> This is the afterlife of slavery – skewed life chances, limited access to health and education, premature death, incarceration, and impoverishment. I, too, am the afterlife of slavery.

True enough, Hobsbawm's[47] discussion dwells on the relationship between industrial capitalism, nationalism and imperialism, but even then cannot much advance on Williams' path-breaking study *Capitalism and Slavery*, which charted not only how the 'commercial capitalism of the eighteenth century developed the wealth of Europe by means of slavery and monopoly', but also how this 'helped to create the industrial capitalism of the nineteenth century'[48] which is so central to Hobsbawm's later accounts of nationalism. The latter author, moreover, had virtually nothing to say of the manifestation or legacy of these histories in British culture and society. There are important resources carried in Anderson in this respect, not only that nation-states are a recent cultural artefact (so that – as previously stated – nationalism creates nations, not the other way around[49]), but also his argument that 'racism dreams of eternal contaminations'[50] in the making of nations as imagined communities. An implication is that these features can be imagined-out just as much as they are imagined-in. To think this plausible is to direct attention to the fleetingly discussed 'turbulent histories', and bring to the centre those stories that, following Moses:

> situate the racial violence on the imperial periphery, essential for the retention of European dominance in the nineteenth century, as part of the same flow of events that led to the eruption of violence in Europe in 1914 and again a quarter of a century later. In this way, the genocidal episodes of the 'racial century' are linked in a complex causal nexus of upwardly spiralling violence against real and imagined threats to the viability of marginal nation-states.[51]

If we consider what Berman characterised as 'classical modernity',[52] the period after the French Revolution (1789–1900) and the long 19th century that saw the birth of industrial capitalism in Europe, it quickly becomes apparent that colonialisation and imperial systems of wealth and labour extraction from the Global South were a keystone of European nation-state formation.[53] That, between them, the Spanish, Portuguese, British, French and Belgium empires could annex and appropriate the human beings, materials resources and knowledge systems of the entire African continent, large swathes of South and East Asia, Australasia and Latin and Central America, and this *not* underpin nation-state formation is a view sustained only by omission.[54] The ways in which European empires went about this varies, of course, something reflected in how the subsequent colonial rule took different forms. The mutilating indentured labour of the Congolese by the Belgians, the creation of a compliant British imperial Raj, as well as the mass exterminations that accompanied settler societies and colonies of North America and Australasia, offer diverging examples of coloniality and imperial governance.[55] The important point is that European imperialism is both *preceded* and *proceeded* by the period of 'classical modernity' and European nation-state formation, and to read this entire period as external to the very constitution of European nation-states is to actively foreclose any possibility that a 'long imperial hegemony, and the intimacy of the relationship between capitalist development at home and colonial conquest overseas, laid the trace of an active racism in it'.[56]

So, there are two key points here. The first is that prevailing accounts of European nation-state formation, whether proposed by modernists, ethno-symbolists or primordialists, have largely overlooked the role of imperialism and colonialism, not least 'the exterminatory dimension of nation-building'.[57] The second is that this tendency has obscured the ways in which, to quote Wolfe, 'reciprocally, colonialism subsequently came to furnish a racialised mythology that could be displaced back onto stigmatised minorities within Europe itself'.[58] Each of these are important not only as historical accounts in and of themselves, but also for understanding racial injustice today, and specifically how 'past wrongs in present circumstances includes future-oriented considerations about improving the situation that resulted from them'.[59]

Memory holes

Perhaps in the final analysis the argument being mobilised here asks us to grasp how scholarship that has been 'elaborated within the confines of Western modernity' retains its ethnocentric anchorage.[60] The objective of this complaint is not to devalue this scholarship; it is instead to seek an understanding of its relationship to colonialism, and the ways in which they 'are already deeply implicated within each other'.[61] This is why the designation 'post-' can be misleading, for the challenge that postcolonial and decolonial enquiry variously presents is not only anchored in what 'turbulent histories' happened *after* decolonisation, but also on the form and content of colonialism and its subsequent (indeed contemporary) implications.

It is important to be clear what is being argued here for, as previously insisted, the social dynamics of racial injustice in our present moment cannot merely be 'read off' these historical currents, for the process of racialisation is also contingent even while there are necessarily shared racial mechanisms.[62]

The concern signalled in the previous chapter, and returned to throughout this book, is that even while the *mechanics of racialisation* share common properties, they necessarily operate differently in curating and sustaining diverse racial projects. What is being claimed in this chapter is more minimal: specifically, that imperialism was constitutive of European nation-state formation in ways that have implications for how national identities are presently imagined. In this respect there is a continuing dialogue between the colonial and the postcolonial and decolonial. This sounds like a contradictory statement until we grasp that alongside symbols are other vestiges of imperialism; the economic assets, and built environments, the very laws that govern our societies bear their imprint – and chief among these: our very criteria of citizenship.[63]

We can illustrate this point by noting how only a generation after its height, when it claimed jurisdiction over a quarter of the planet's population, Britain would become a nation-state with the introduction of British Nationality Act 1948. Henceforth, colonial 'British subjects' became Citizens of the United Kingdom and Colonies (CUKCs). Without wishing to list a chronology documented elsewhere,[64] Britain's post-imperial story can partly be read through its subsequent immigration legislation, commencing with the Commonwealth Immigrants Act 1962 and followed by the hastily passed Commonwealth Immigrants Act 1968 (designed to prevent the entry of fleeing Kenyan and other African Asians holding British citizenship). The Immigration Act 1971 meanwhile partly enshrined a *jus sanguinis* type of legal citizenship, based upon ethnic descent, through the introduction of a 'partiality' clause. Accordingly, a person seeking entry from the Commonwealth would need to demonstrate that a parent or grandparent had been born in the UK. This meant that 'new' Commonwealth citizens (of the West Indies, South Asia and East Africa) would be less likely than 'old' Commonwealth citizens (of Australia or Canada) to qualify for entry. The Nationality Act 1981 tried to delineate this further through the creation of three categories of British citizenship: (i) British Citizen, (ii) British Dependent Territories Citizen or (iii) British Overseas Citizen, and ultimately withdrew a right to settlement from most Commonwealth citizens.

While a suite of further migration legislation was introduced throughout the subsequent decades, what is important to note is how 'colonial citizens' (under the terms of the CUKC) would become coded out of subsequent iterations of a substantive British Citizenship, such that 'populations that would, historically, have been part of the body politic'[65] were placed outside it as the ground cruelly shifted under their feet. This 'migrantisation'[66] of erstwhile British citizens became especially visible in the ongoing Windrush scandal. Here, a number of the children of Black Britons who came from the Caribbean between 1948 and 1973, and who were legally entitled to all the rights that came with full membership of the nation-state, have seen the citizenship rights rescinded. Particularly important was the Nationality, Immigration and Asylum Act 2002, which introduced policies requiring non-state agencies to share information with the Home Office, expanding the power to deprive people of citizenship, and this was vigorously pursued through the self-designated 'Hostile Environment' policy approach to immigration reflected in the 2014 and 2016 Immigration Acts. The key point is that none of this would have been plausible unless there was an underlying racial project that rationalised this approach, and a racist social system that operationalised it.

Many of those affected had moved to the UK as CUKCs before their birth countries became independent, and for any number of reasons may not have applied for a British passport. Their stories are too numerous and rich to be summarised; they included people like Paulette Wilson, who 'had been in Britain from the age of 10, worked, raised a family and should have been enjoying her retirement, but she'd had her liberty taken away and been threatened with deportation back to Jamaica – a country she hardly knew'.[67] Another is the case of Nathaniel:

> In 2001, Nathaniel went on holiday to Jamaica with his daughter Veronica. Little did either of them know that Nathaniel would never see the UK again. When they set off to come home to the UK, immigration authorities told him he would not be allowed back into the country. The passport he had had for some

45 years, which declared him a Citizen of the UK and Colonies, was no longer good enough, though it had been in 1985, when he last made the trip. And it had been in the mid-1950s, when he arrived in the UK as a young man, in common with thousands of other men, women and children, members of what we now know as the Windrush generation. Nine years after his holiday, Nathaniel died in Jamaica, unable to afford treatment for prostate cancer. He and Veronica had decided not to fight the original decision against him. Instead, she had taken career breaks to look after him in Jamaica. Nathaniel's story, and Veronica's, are part of what we have come to call the Windrush scandal.[68]

The challenge of estimating the true number of people who might have been affected was noted by the National Audit Office (NAO) in its 2018 report into the Windrush scandal.[69] The NAO refers to analysis conducted by the Home Office in 2014, and estimates that there could be 500,000 people in the UK who would struggle to document their status. Given that the UK Home Office has never formally or systematically issued documentation to this group, it is not possible to ascertain precisely the number of people who remain undocumented, and therefore the full scale of those affected. Perhaps this is best viewed as something akin to Orwell's memory hole, that useful mechanism for the alteration or disappearance of inconvenient or embarrassing documents, photographs, transcripts, or other records as part of an attempt to give the impression that something never happened.[70] In another way, the Windrush scandal is an illustration of Valluvan's insistence that 'if one basic proposition about what constitutes nationalism is to be advanced', this will be found in 'the relationship between political discourse, ideology and nation'.[71] He continues: 'Namely, western nationalism can be read as the formation by which a self-appointed normative community attributes its putative socioeconomic, cultural and security concerns to the excessive presence and allowance made to those understood as not belonging.'

This is a pertinent reading, for while it is, of course, true that nationalism studies are not of one kind, it is also true that the field reflects a profoundly unsatisfactory engagement with race, empire and its implications.[72] It would be unkind to characterise an interdisciplinary field, one with so much invested in historical analysis, as an intellectual example of Wekker's description of 'white innocence'.[73] The charge instead is that it has seen too little in racial histories of nation-state formation, and this is self-evidently a problem, not least because Empire has been constitutive of nation-state formation, something that in Britain came 'home' long before *Windrush* docked in Tilbury. The missed opportunities to recognise and engage with this are the source of a continuing frustration in race scholarship.

Remaking 'Britishness'?

Conversely, if scholars of nations and nationalism have been insufficiently interested in race, we might say that for a long time some prominent scholars of race were insufficiently uninterested in national identity. Part of the reason for the latter may be the long shadow cast by how, after the war, and inspired by the Chicago sociologists, a very British take on 'race relations' flourished through the work of Banton,[74] Glass,[75] Patterson,[76] Rex and Moore[77] and Rose,[78] but to whom remaking national membership was not a concern. As we revisit in the following chapter, their impact was evident in a number of respects, not least when the Labour government introduced minimal measures to address direct racial discrimination; something which proceeded through the introduction of a Race Relations Act (in 1965). Why it was not, for example, called the 'Anti-Racism Act' is instructive, for it partly reflected the continuing influence of Park's view that the relations within which discrimination occurs must be those of race relations.[79] This is a familiar account that does not need to be rehearsed here. Suffice to say that Banton's book, simply called *Race Relations*, is indicative of this way of thinking and serves as a useful illustration of how approaches in this period were being framed.[80]

What is noteworthy is the charge put forward by critics that these authors did not offer sustained analyses of questions of power, and were consequently 'atheoretical' and 'ahistorical', 'concerned with 'attitudes', 'prejudice' and 'discrimination' and were 'remarkably uninformative'.[81] Rex's work[82] most certainly eschewed a narrow focus by pointing to the importance of social and economic marginalisation, yet he appeared unable to integrate these sociological concerns into 'wider conceptual debates about the theory of racism or into the analysis of processes of racialization in contemporary Britain'.[83] It is especially interesting that Bob Miles would later claim that his work did not entail as much a rejection of what preceded him as may have previously been claimed. In relation to Banton, he reflects on how he '"hijacked" his [Banton's] concept of racialization because to me it spoke to a process. And what he was good at researching and writing about was historical processes by which the idea of "race" took meanings in different contexts'.[84] Beyond this, his interest in nationhood was focused principally on the tension between 'the need of the capitalist world economy for the mobility of human beings, and on the other, the drawing of territorial boundaries and the construction of citizenship as a legal category which sets boundaries for human mobility'.[85]

All of this remains relevant because one pivot in thinking about national identity came in response to these framings, which were said to limit the scope of theory and silence racial subjects.[86] As Hall would later conclude, 'these fundamentally binary terms in which British race relations have been mapped have essentially collapsed',[87] an assessment informed by (as well as informing) the 'new ethnicities' problematic. This sought to engage the shifting complexities of ethnic identities, specifically their processes of formation and change, something given an authoritative voice in the work of Hall.[88] A different iteration of the same concern can be found in Modood's (1992) *Not Easy Being British: Culture, Colour and Citizenship*,[89] which marked an important intervention with the author probably the first social scientist to get beyond the binary rhetoric of being for or against Salman Rushdie's *The Satanic Verses*. He did this by placing the UK Muslim mobilisations within a register of minority claim-making (rather than blasphemy or religious offence). The intervention challenged antiracists to recognise

Muslim minorities, rather than dismiss them as being anti-Enlightenment zealots, and included Modood's insistence on the need for concepts of race and racism that could critique sociocultural environments which devalue people because of physical differences but also because of membership of a cultural minority.[90] Critically, he argued, the two often overlap and create a double disadvantage (including on the grounds of religious identity). To grasp this, he maintained, requires an account 'that is able to connect a group's internal structure, values and understanding of itself ... with how that group is categorised and treated as a subordinate race within wider society'.[91]

In many respects, these new ethnicities approaches marked a timely intellectual development that captured the ways in which 'identities had broken free of their anchorage in singular histories of race and nation',[92] and corresponded with what the commentator Alibhai-Brown characterised as an optimistic period in which Britain was prepared to take stock and 'assess whether existing cultural and political edifices are keeping up with the people and the evolving habitat'.[93] This came at the turn of the millennium, and after 18 long years of Conservative rule, a Labour government was still in its first term with a large Parliamentary majority and political capital to spend. This was an overdue opening to rethink the national story beyond a kind of insider/outsider relationship, something more akin to an upward spiral out of an entrenched setting. As the previous chapter signalled, and the next chapter focuses on further, the commissioners leading the Stephen Lawrence Inquiry felt it had raised sufficient public consciousness to reflect on institutional racism, and the government declared a commitment to creating a country where racial diversity was 'celebrated'. These sentiments were thrown into sharp relief by the immediate reaction to the *Report of the Commission on the Future of Multi-Ethnic Britain*.

Central to the report by the Commission's chair, the political philosopher Bhikhu Parekh, was the idea that there is a difference between the identities of nations and people's national identities – and that if anything, the former had to catch up with the latter. By this, Parekh and the other commissioners meant that the formal representation of a country ought to be reconfigured so as to reflect the identifications of its people –

shifting in Britain's case from a laissez-faire 'multicultural drift' to a concerted recognition of how postcolonial Britons had remade Britain. The clue was in the title *The Future of Multi-Ethnic Britain* – a conversation that might add to and expand the racial equality discourses of the 1980s in ways that shifted some of the burden of change onto White majorities too. The implicit argument was that minority cultures, norms and symbols have as much right as their hegemonic counterparts to state provision and public space, and to be recognised as members of groups if sought. Perhaps just as importantly, however, and as Stuart Hall who sat on the commission put it, this was a story of change:

> We described the growing tendency for ethnic minority people to identify themselves as Black-British or British-Asian as a positive sign of their 'claim to belong'. But belonging is a tricky concept, requiring both identification and recognition.[94]

In other words, the 'problem' of national identity rested not with Black and ethnic minorities, it was White majorities and the state that needed to catch up. For Hall, as for other commissioners, the challenge was to take account of 'inescapable changes', including post-war migration, the end of empire, devolution and globalisation. To this end, the report made over 140 policy recommendations to encourage 'a confident and vibrant multicultural society' to take advantage of 'its rich diversity' in order that Britain should realise its full potential.[95] It strongly endorsed both the possibility and desirability of forging a meta-membership of 'Britishness', but simply one that recognised the stories and contributions of ethnic and racial minorities too. Its recommendations sought to prevent discrimination or overcome its effects, and championed an approach that could move beyond conceptions of formal equality by recognising the substantive elements of 'real differences of experience, background and perception'.[96] For example, the CMEB advocated a systematic type of ethnic monitoring that would 'go beyond racism and culture blind strategies',[97] and could be implemented across public institutions to promote a recognition of cultural diversity in general, and 'unwitting' discrimination in particular. It claimed that while high-profile statements of ideals by senior politicians and civil servants are not unimportant in framing agendas, 'they remain mere paper commitments or rhetoric, however, if they are not fully incorporated into all mainstream agendas and programmes'.[98]

Revisiting the report more than 20 years later reveals an attempt to reconcile a changing national identity with an honest and necessary account of its origins; to forge a country that did not disenfranchise its Black and ethnic minorities. This is why the Commission recommended that central government take steps in formally declaring Britain a multicultural society – it was hoped that such an approach would begin to steer a new course in imagining national identity.[99] A question we might nonetheless ask today is: Was it naive, too celebratory? It certainly reflected a cumulative political movement that had followed the migrations of the parents and grandparents of many of Britain's post-immigrant ethnic minorities, who had exercised their Commonwealth citizenship and journeyed to its metropole. If the shameful Windrush deportations tell us nothing else, it is that any meaningful sense of national belonging for many Black and minority ethnic Britons will remain unachieved unless the country is able to recognise its imperial moorings. The observation, of course, had long been made, at least since Hall had previously argued that:

> A decisive mental repression … has overtaken the British people about race and Empire since the 1950s. Paradoxically, it seems to me, the native home grown variety of racism begins with this attempt to wipe out and efface every trace of the colonial and imperial past.[100]

Yet there is seemingly sufficient resonance of Empire in the nation's life to encourage Her Majesty's Treasury to send a 'Friday Fact tweet' that 'Millions of you helped end the slave trade through your taxes'.[101] In this instance, the British government could take pride in abolition, but not responsibility for slavery's expansion nor the colossal wealth and horror this entailed. As Hartman has argued in her account of 'incidental death', this inability reflects the ranking of racialised subjects below matters of commerce. She elaborates:

> Incidental death occurs when life has no normative value, when no humans are involved, when the population is, in effect, seen as already dead. Unlike the concentration camp, the gulag, and the killing field, which had as their intended end the extermination of a population, the Atlantic trade created millions of corpses, but as a corollary to the making of commodities.[102]

Why might things be different when 43 per cent of people polled by YouGov can take pride in Britain's history of colonialism and deem it 'something to be proud of' in the present?[103] One view maintains that such instances emerge from a form of postcolonial melancholia, something which 'blinds us to the connections between race thinking and the white supremacism that legitimized colonial endeavour, so much so that we fail to notice that racism is a problem until the next tragic death or inflammatory eruption shakes us temporarily out of our complacency'.[104] This is not, of course, unique to Britain, and in his account of *Why the French Don't Like Headscarves*, John Bowen picks up this thread in relation to France's refusal to recognise its colonial and postcolonial implications, arguing that even though the Muslim headscarves and mosques are not objectively more visible than other religious difference, they are subjectively shocking because they force White French people to think about how being French is no longer – if it ever was – the preserve of White Christians.[105] In our case, this key historical point was overlooked in the clamour at the time to decry the Parekh report as an assault on national identity, specifically focusing on the report's central observation that the idea of Britishness carried 'largely unspoken racial connotations'. The *Daily Telegraph*'s Philip Johnston accused the commissioners of wanting to 'rewrite our history', all the while failing to see it was an attempt to share and take ownership for history.[106] As McCarthy has argued, the distribution of this task sits at the very foundation of what must be erected upon it, since:

> Each generation of citizens, whether native- or
> foreign-born, inherits the burdens of membership
> – the national debts, as it were – together with the
> benefits of membership ... This is not a matter of
> collective guilt but of collective responsibility; and
> reparation is not a matter of collective punishment
> but of collective liability.[107]

While perhaps an inevitable response from the right, the CMEB
also incurred the wrath of prominent liberals who considered
its approach a grave challenge to liberalism, not least those
recommendations in it which promoted diversity as a feature
of equality.[108] As discussed in the following chapter, this is a
longstanding impediment in political liberalism, and at the time
none other than Lord Anthony Lester, one of the founders of the
Runnymede Trust and a key architect of Britain's race equality
legislation, said of the report that: 'Much of the more theoretical
sections is written entirely from the perspective of victims.'[109]
This and other liberal reactions illustrate how the exclusion
that comes with majority cultural precedence is often sustained
by a broad coalition among racial majorities from seemingly
different political traditions. The Home Secretary, Jack Straw,
meanwhile, went lukewarm on learning of the backlash, and
eventually attacked the report's recommendations, in line with
the Middle-England electorate whom Labour seemed unwilling
to confront. The report warned us that institutional and
personally mediated racism had cultivated systemic inequality
that needed to be recognised. Institutional racism then, just as
now, 'unwittingly' allowed White people to gain more from the
education system, the criminal justice system, the labour market,
and the health system, while also affording marginal attention
to the racial dimensions of policy responses in these sectors.
It was precisely in these areas that the report recommended
measurable interventions.

'Fundamental British values'

What is described has been neither a linear nor a stable
development, and has frequently been resisted. Two decades

since the Parekh report, a period that has included civil disturbances, illegal wars abroad and terrorism at home, as well as the distinctively multicultural London 2012 Olympics, the core idea that Britishness has been remade by Black and minority ethnic Britons is hard to erase even if it is resisted. This appears not only in the self-definitions of minorities but also in the discursive formation of the Britishness writ large – while neither are complete or settled, they are profoundly important multicultural successes that must not be ignored.[110] Indeed, it might even be argued that the precarious status of Britishness is, somewhat ironically, better observed in debates about devolution and constitutional settlements, in which it remains an open question as to where multicultural difference fits in these contexts.[111]

This is then to register the persistence of claims-making on the national identity of Britishness, through an agent-centred contestation. Such moves, as Baldwin put it,[112] understand that to 'accept one's past – one's history – is not the same thing as drowning in it; it is learning how to use it'. None of this should not be taken to imply that racial criteria for membership of the nation have dissolved, nor that minorities are not viewed as an indication of national decline. For, in many respects, it is an asymmetrical recognition: one abundantly apparent to ethnic and racial minorities, and oftentimes White majorities too, but not yet among the political actors nor the systems they use to govern. Gilroy's prediction that 'it will take far more than the will to create a "pluralist national identity" to prise the jaws of the bulldog of British nationalism free',[113] describe an ongoing task. This is not only about continuity, however, for, consistent with the argument made so far, present racial projects are not a replication of what Lawrence had to say of the Britishness of the 1970s, specifically that 'the "alien" cultures of the blacks ... was as either the cause or else the most visible symptom of the destruction of the "British way of life"'.[114] Instead, the issue in contemporary restatements of Britishness shares common mechanics with what has proceeded, particularly in pointing to Muslim difference as a threat to the nation. This has been most consistently elaborated in the UK government's promotion of 'fundamental British values' (FBV).[115] Clearly, issues here around 'values' are complex, not only in themselves, but also in terms of how they are used as a basis for national identification.

Applying an understanding of racial systems and projects invites us to explore how, in such moves, a latent Whiteness provides a series of racialised cultural codes that undergird public policy norms. For, rather than the possibility of remaking national identity in the manner proposed in the Parekh report, the Coalition government (2010–15) specifically emphasised Britishness as a means of preventing terrorism, something that has come to define integration talk – or, specifically, not integrating in the proscribed fashion. For example, the idea of FBV now assumes a prominent place in the English National Curriculum and elsewhere, and constitutes part of 'Spiritual, Moral, Social and Cultural' development (SMSC) in schools.[116] It is reminiscent of Mosse's calibration of racism and nationalism through the example of prescribed national character, for 'if racism constructed an ideal type, nationalism was sooner or later in search of the proper 'national character ... if nations identified a national character in a consistent manner, then nationalism and racism drew much closer together'.[117] It is particularly notable that FBV actually first appears in political discourse in 2011 within the definition of 'extremism', and is outlined in the government's counterterrorism Prevent Strategy as follows:

> Extremism is vocal or active opposition to fundamental British values, including democracy, the rule of law, individual liberty and mutual respect and tolerance of different faiths and beliefs. We also include in our definition of extremism calls for the death of members of our armed forces, whether in this country or overseas.[118]

In its provenance, then, FBV was anchored in a focus on security which folded counterterrorism criteria aimed at Muslim communities into an allegedly universal basis for membership. What is described here is more active than 'coming to the game after it is already begun, after the rules and standards have been set, and having to prove oneself accordingly'.[119] A more active, novel and sustained use of national identity is in operation, to single out and target, wielding the full security apparatus of the state, an existing body of its citizenry. It is for this reason that the chapter implores us to engage with our past in order to cultivate a meaningful version of our present and future. The very notion of Whiteness, as a structured norm against which others are valued less, has for too long received scant attention in the study of nations and nationalism. There are tools to remedy this, especially in ways that allow us to consider how societies push 'nationalisms' to the periphery of social life, making it something that happens elsewhere and not here, amongst us. Yet these, too, are disinterested in how and why the social processes are ensconced by racially imaginaries. In his book *Banal Nationalism*,[120] Billig encouraged readers to recognise something analogous to this, and reorient their focus by attempting:

> to look beyond the dialogues of conscious sense-making towards a psychology of the unnoticed. The flags hanging in the street, or attached to the lapels of politicians, carry no propositional message for the ordinary citizen to receive passively or consciously argue against. Yet, such symbols help us to maintain the everyday world as belonging to the world of nation-states.[121]

He argued that this encourages the view that nationalism has gone away and then returns – that it is a latent force that manifests itself like a natural disaster which strikes spontaneously and unpredictably, famously described by Gellner as the 'Dark Gods theory of nationalism'.[122] For Billig, this approach misunderstands nationalism as something spectacular, and misses its subtler manifestations – ignoring how we all participate in sustaining it for different ends. Symbols in this way can act as 'border guards', and are 'linked to specific cultural codes and function to identify people as members or non-members of the specific national collectivity'.[123]

What these accounts appear disinclined to explore are the ways in which the very same impulses may be anchored in 'racially framed meanings, racial practices, racial hierarchy, and racial power networks and structures created and maintained by whites'.[124] At best, there may be an allowance to describe instances of racial injustice, but an unwillingness to attribute any benefit to and from what preserves it. The arguments presented in this chapter have been that in order to pursue something to the contrary requires naming racial inequalities and not pretending these are an aberration in an otherwise race-less, meritocratic society – by truly learning about our colonial history and jettisoning myths about Britain doing everything on its own and against the odds. As Baldwin once put it, 'People who imagine that history flatters them … become incapable of seeing or changing themselves or the world'.[125] The alternative invites us to take ownership of racial inequalities as part of our story as a society, and to do so without being defensive, and it is to these inequalities that we turn next.

THREE

Equality, inequalities and institutional racism

How do we tackle racial injustice not self-evidently sustained by individual motives alone, nor formally supported in public policy? This is what is at the heart of institutional racism – something that draws our focus to conventions and away from stated objectives in the continuation and proliferation of racial inequality. One word that relates to what is being described here is 'unwitting', and this is precisely how institutional racism came to be understood in an inquiry into the London Metropolitan Police Force. This followed a long campaign by the parents of the teenager Stephen Lawrence who was murdered in the course of a racist attack in 1993 by a group of young White men. In the official inquiry undertaken by Sir William Macpherson, the investigating judge found the Metropolitan Police Force, the largest police force in the country, guilty of 'unwitting racism' that was nonetheless anchored in its prevailing institutional practice. The inquiry made a number of wide-ranging recommendations that reflected, perhaps for the first time in Britain, an official recognition of the endemic character of racism within a core public institution. Fast forward more than a quarter of a century since Stephen Lawrence's killing, and what can we say was achieved – either partially or wholly – and what objectives did we fall short of, and why?

Talking and legislating

To answer these questions, we need to recognise that one of the many paradoxes of racial injustice in Britain is that while the kinds of disavowal of racism discussed in the previous chapter are pervasive, public discourse has long been gripped by 'race talk'. This refers to what Lewis has described as a 'metalanguage through which other axes of power, which organize social relations and construct positions are at once spoken and masked'.[1] Nothing is without its history, and so 'race talk' might be evident at various points in time, but a good place to begin in public policy is more than half a century ago when the Conservative parliamentarian Enoch Powell made his infamous 'Rivers of Blood' speech to the West Midlands Area Conservative Political Association in 1968.[2] While Powell himself partly set his speech against international events, especially the US civil rights movement, his immediate catalyst was almost certainly the Labour Government's Race Relations Bill which was due to receive its second reading only three days after his intervention.[3] That Bill, as enacted, now forms part of an incremental race equality architecture which tried to address some of the weaknesses of its more voluntarist 1965 predecessor, explicitly making unlawful forms of discrimination on grounds of colour, race or ethnic or national origins in employment, housing and the provision of commercial and other services.

Importantly, when it came into effect, the 1968 Act also created a forerunner to the later Commission for Racial Equality (CRE) in the shape of the Race Relations Board, which was charged with ensuring compliance with the legislation's provisions, but also with investigating complaints of discriminatory behaviour and supporting legal proceedings. That the prospect of this legislation especially animated Powell was reflected in his characterisation of it as 'one-way privilege' and 'a match on to the gunpowder'.[4] 'The kindest thing that can be said about those who propose and support it', he continued, 'is that they know not what they do.' It is safe to assume that Powell was not making a comment on the potential weaknesses in the proposed Bill relative to its stated ambition, for it was soon after considered insufficient in the area of labour-market participation, where indirect discrimination remained unchallenged. As such, a subsequent Labour Government committed to revising the legislation in the 1976 Race Relations Bill, stating 'the Government is convinced, as a result of its review of race relations generally and of the working of the legislation, that a fuller strategy to deal with racial disadvantage will have to be deployed than has been attempted so far'.[5] Indeed, it is now over 45 years since the introduction of this third Race Relations Act (in 1976) cemented a state sponsorship of race equality by consolidating and then expanding the earlier, weaker legislative instruments (the 1965 and 1968 Race Relations Acts). Alongside a remit spanning public and private institutions, recognition of indirect discrimination and the imposition of a statutory public duty to promote 'good race relations', the 1976 Act also created the CRE to monitor implementation to assist individual complainants. As such it marked an important moment in an evolving settlement, for it recognised that Citizens of the United Kingdom and Colonies (CUKCs) and their British-born children were encountering a social system in which racial barriers were routinely in place.

Notably, 1968, the year of Powell's speech, was also the year of the Commonwealth Immigrants Bill which would specifically restrict entry, as the previous chapter discussed, to those who had at least one parent or grandparent born here (and so favouring migrants from White majority 'Commonwealth' settler societies such as Australian, Canada and New Zealand). As a young Liberal parliamentarian, David Steel argued at the time that the move marked 'an attempt to write into British law legislation that discriminated between citizens on the grounds of race, and which represented a grave breach of international and internal political obligations'.[6] Of course, Powell's speech was no less relevant to this Immigration Bill than to the Race Relations Bill, and the speech was even credited with setting the Labour Government's immigration agenda. As the pre-Rupert Murdoch *Times* editorial put it on the morning of the passing of the Immigration Act 1968, 'What is the government so afraid of? Is it afraid of Mr Enoch Powell? ... It is probably the most shameful measure that Labour members have ever been asked by their whips to support.'[7]

A self-evident relationship then has existed between the policy objectives of race equality and migration control, and remains a characteristic of 'race talk' in Britain since Powell. It is constitutive of a tension that is unsettled and periodically reveals itself, as illustrated by the Windrush injustices. Nonetheless, and despite some very opportune moments over the years, the formal race equality legislation was never repealed but expanded, and later developed, through a patchwork approach, into the Equality Act 2010, which brought together (and levelled up) a number of protected 'grounds' of which race was one (together with gender, disability, age, sexuality, religion, marital status, and so on). Less positively, this later development was accompanied by the absorption of the CRE into a newly created Equality and Human Rights Commission (EHRC) that would radically reduce a dedicated focus on racial injustice.

While most certainly not unproblematic then, these kinds of developments set out a markedly different approach to that of neighbouring European countries with recent colonial histories. For example, during its experience of significant post-colonial settlement, France pursued a robustly assimilationist strategy in which equality was understood as uniformity and, until the beginning of this millennium, Germany maintained a returnist approach in which labour migrants were guest-workers (*gastarbeiter*) expected to return to their country of origin. In the UK, despite the traction of Powell and Powellites, and under the remit of the kinds of race equality legislation previously discussed, there developed a formal approach to equal opportunity conceived as equal access to the labour market and other key spheres of British society (for example, education, health and political participation). Against this background, the relevant question is always: have these approaches been successful?

The long tail of racial inequalities

Much, of course, depends on the criteria of relevance. If the intended objective of the initial and later race equality legislation was to reduce ethnic and racial disparities to a marginal or 'negligible' level, then the answer is most certainly not. For, drawing on a variety of openly available sources, including the race disparity audit,[8] we quickly see that among the most salient ethnic and racial inequalities across the UK, Black and minority ethnic households are twice as likely to be in persistent poverty as White households.[9] Indeed, and Achiume, acting as the UN Special Rapporteur on contemporary forms of racism, racial discrimination, xenophobia and related intolerance, has highlighted how these have continued in plain sight, witnessed in the disproportionate impact on racial minorities of broader inequalities emerging in recent years:

> [T]he racially disparate impact of austerity measures adopted by the government between 2010 and 2017 will result in a 5% loss of income for black households, which is double the loss for white households. Similarly, cash losses ... as a result of tax, welfare and wage reforms will be the largest for black households (about £1,600 average) and the smallest for white households (about £950 average).[10]

As somebody who convened an expert group on Scotland to feed into the race disparity audit, the findings that the UN mission reported only confirmed our existing knowledge: specifically, that very significant ethnic and racial disparities continue to feature across all key sectors of British society and that, contrary to the expectation of incremental progress, in a number of respects they are getting worse. An overview restatement of these data might include how one quarter of Black and Asian children, compared with one tenth of White children, are likely to be in persistent poverty,[11] and that the unemployment rate for Black-African and Black-Caribbean groups across the UK is more than twice the national average, while Pakistani and Bangladeshi groups have an unemployment rate of 10 per cent compared with 4 per cent for White groups.[12] This finding was previously recognised by the EHRC,[13] and confirmed a trend signalled in Trades Union Congress research that highlighted how 45 per cent of Black 16–24-year-olds were unemployed, which is over double the level of unemployment of their White counterparts. Meanwhile, Black and minority ethnic employees with degrees earned 23.1 per cent less on average than White workers with comparable education and training,[14] and, as Bowyer and colleagues have shown, Black and ethnic minority young people are 47 per cent more likely to be on a zero hours contract, compared to their White peers.[15]

The reasons for this are both simple and complex, but invariably reflect the work of racial projects in social systems.

In their study using data from field studies on labour market discrimination, set against the UK Labour Force Survey for comparable groups, Zwysen, Di Stasio and Heath have convincingly documented 'a sizeable positive relation between the degree of ethnic discrimination recorded in field experiments and the overall disadvantage faced by ethnic minorities on the labour market'.[16] They conclude that this 'strongly suggests that ethnic penalties reflect hiring discrimination, and generally groups that experience worse hiring discrimination also have higher ethnic penalties in employment'.[17] The findings in these studies continue to elaborate a pattern first identified by Daniel[18] in, for example, the *then* extent of unemployment among 'West Indian' and 'Asian' men – in spite of the fact that it was labour shortages that had brought people to this country (but who came as *citizens*, and would be later turned into *migrants* through the creation of successive immigration legislation).

For more than 50 years, researchers in the US and the UK examining racial discrimination have had in their armoury the use of field experiments, the so-called 'matched pairs method'. What has flowed from this work is a literature from field experiments that illustrate how job applicants from minority ethnic and racial groups in the UK are, other things being equal, less likely to receive a positive reply to their application than White British majority applicants. Subsequent research, especially the Policy Studies Institute (PSI) second and third national surveys of ethnic minorities,[19] showed that unemployment and low pay persisted, although the pattern of disadvantage was not uniform. What, however, of the experiences of the children and grandchildren of these pioneer generations? Here we find that, in higher education, for example, among Black African and Black Caribbean groups, just 6 per cent of school leavers attended a Russell Group university, as compared with 11 per cent of White school leavers. As for employment in the university sector, the Equality Challenge Unit's audit showed that nearly 70 per cent of UK professorships are held by White men, while just under 22 per cent are held by White women.[20] Some 7.3 per cent of professors are Black and minority ethnic men, and just 1.9 per cent are Black and minority ethnic women. Among university senior managers, 67.5 per cent are White male, 28.3 per cent are White female, 3.3 per cent are Black and minority ethnic male and only 0.9 per cent are Black and minority ethnic female. Corresponding inquiry from Rollock documents the qualitative character of these discrepancies, and 'the lack of fellow Black academics within universities, especially at senior levels, along with the challenges, delays, racism and passive bullying they have experienced'.[21] These everyday struggles, and negotiations of what Mahtani discusses as emotionally toxic material spaces, are a further illustration of the affective load carried by racial minorities in educational settings today.[22] Elsewhere, and as we revisit in the next chapter with the discussion of COVID-19 risk factors, we know that Pakistani, Bangladeshi and Black adults are more likely to live in substandard accommodation than White people (around 30 per cent compared with around 8 per cent, respectively). Indeed, as the Joseph Rowntree Foundation reported, over the past 20 years:

> working-age people in the White ethnic group have always had the lowest risk of poverty, with those from the Indian group having the second lowest. Those in the Bangladeshi and Pakistani groups have continuously had the highest and second highest poverty rates respectively, with the people in the Black, and Chinese and Other ethnic groups having similar rates.[23]

Given the disproportionate impact of austerity measures already highlighted, and regarding ethnic and racial minority women in particular, there is every reason to anticipate that this disparity has increased. This is signalled by findings from the EHRC,[24] in which the UN Rapporteur stated that 'children from Pakistani or Bangladeshi households (28.6 per cent) and Black households (24.2 per cent) were more likely to live in substandard accommodation than those in White households (18.6 per cent)'.[25] It is also related to the status of homeownership reported in the race disparity audit, which showed how, in England in 2015–17, Black African and Black Caribbean households were the ethnic groups most likely to rent social housing (47 per cent and 45 per cent, respectively).[26]

The disparities that are found in the labour market, higher education and housing sectors reappear in areas such as formal and informal school exclusions and criminal justice, where in England, Black children are more likely to be permanently excluded than White British pupils.[27] The Lammy Review meanwhile highlighted the over-representation of Gypsy, Roma and Traveller children in secure centres, as well as a striking increase in Muslim prisoners across different ethnicities from about 8,900 to 13,200 over the past decade.[28] Indeed, in the area of criminal justice more broadly, rates of prosecution for Black African and African Caribbean people are three times higher than for White people – 18 per thousand of the population compared with six per thousand, respectively.[29] Black people make up 3 per cent of the UK population but accounted for 12 per cent of the adult prison population.[30] Other minoritised groups were also over-represented but to a lesser degree, for the experience of Black groups typically outstrips that of others, as further shown by Joseph-Salisbury, Connelly and Wangari-Jones in their account of contemporary British policing:

> Black people are almost ten times more likely to be stopped than White people.... Under certain powers, this harassment becomes even worse. For instance, under 'Section 60' [6] – which allows police officers to search anyone in a defined area for a limited period of time without the requirement of 'reasonable suspicion' – Black people outside of London are 43 times more likely to be stopped and searched than White people ...[31]

The experiences that such racial inequalities illustrate have a long tail, and are another way in which we need to get beyond novelty – the issues are not new simply because they recur. The PSI studies referred to earlier are especially illustrative in this respect for, nearly two generations later, studies which tested for racial discrimination in recruitment processes in British cities showed that 'people from ethnic minorities were less likely to be successful with their applications, even discounting differences such as age and education'.[32] While this relates only to the shortlisting, at the early stage of the recruitment process, in order to secure a job interview the researchers had to send out 74 per cent more applications for minority ethnic candidates compared to White candidates. When they controlled for other factors the researchers attributed this to having a name associated with a Black and minority ethnic background. Building on this work, what Zwysen and colleagues have shown are the ways to gauge – using odds ratios – the probability of a positive response from the employer (ethnic discrimination) or the probability of being employed (ethnic penalty).[33] One clear finding they report is that all minoritised groups are substantially less likely than the White British group to receive a positive call-back when applying for a job. This is not uniform. In their analysis, 'ethnic penalties vary more between non-white groups, however, with Indian, Chinese and other Asian minorities having better labour market outcomes (lower ethnic penalties) than other minority groups who face similar levels of hiring discrimination in the field experiments'.[34] Black African minorities, in particular, stand out as faring least well, both in terms of discrimination and ethnic penalties, and this further reinforces something well established in a variety of literatures. Similar patterns are found outside the UK too. For example, and based on 83,000 applications to real job adverts from over 100 of the largest US employers, a study by Kline and colleagues shows beyond doubt that 'distinctively Black names reduce the probability of employer contact'.[35] Perhaps surprisingly for otherwise reserved economists, their findings move them to call out what they term 'systemic illegal discrimination'.[36] What is true of the labour market is repeated in studies finding that if you have a racial minority background, as reflected in your name, it can affect your chances of obtaining a university place[37] or a rental property.[38]

To be clear, while not all of the disparities experienced by racial minorities can be explained solely by a focus on race and ethnicity, it is simply that systemic inequalities cannot be overlooked in any plausible explanation for them. As Karlsen, Nazroo and Smith have argued in their study of intergenerational economic mobility, '[w]hile there is considerable heterogeneity in these trends, including within particular groups, there is sufficient consistency to suggest that this is a problem produced and perpetuated at the societal level'.[39] A key point is that racial inequalities are not secondary to class or other inequalities: they have distinctive provenance, features and outcomes that need to be recognised. The implication is that since patterns of disadvantage operate societally so must public policy, and specifically in taking group-specific dynamics into account when tackling inequalities.

Liberal obstacles

Among the obstacles to racial justice has long been a resistance to such approaches not only from those hostile to difference.[40] Specifically, there is resistance by liberals to the notion that 'egalitarian principles do seem to require some distinct understanding of the particular needs and forms of exclusion experienced by social groups'.[41] Indeed, liberalism as a political discourse remains incredibly reticent toward recognising the systemic racial inequalities described in this book, and in some respects has not moved a great deal beyond what the American legal theorist Ronald Dworkin set out in his 1978 book *Taking Rights Seriously*.[42] In this he elaborates a distinction between *equal treatment* and *treatment as an equal*. The former tends towards conceiving equality as *uniformity*, while the second is able to take social *characteristics* into consideration. In the past this distinction has been used to argue that 'affirmative action' policies (for example quotas and targets in US college programmes for some minority racial groups) are justified because those groups encounter unfair obstacles in society which prevent them from competing *equally*. This recognition followed the struggle for racial justice described by Martin Luther King as follows: 'the liberal [needs] to see that the oppressed person who agitates for his rights is not the creator of tension. He merely brings out the hidden tension that is already alive'.[43] He elaborates:

> There is nothing abstract about this. It is as concrete as having a good job, a good education, a decent house

and a share of power. It is, however, important to understand that giving a man his due may often mean giving him special treatment. I am aware of the fact that this has been a troublesome concept for many liberals, since it conflicts with their traditional ideal of equal opportunity and equal treatment of people according to their individual merits. But this is a day which demands new thinking and the reevaluation of old concepts.[44]

What is the obstacle, one might ask? One answer returns us to Mills, who has long argued that liberal political theory, because it remains so squarely anchored in a White racial project, sees racism as an exception to the norm:

The sub-discipline whose mission it is to theorize from a normative perspective about personhood and politics, the state and social justice, has made little to no effort to decolonize itself, to reflect upon and rethink its past and present in the light of what are now well-established and uncontroversial facts.[45]

As such, many of the stated advances that have been made in liberal political theory come not from a focus on race and racism, as Scott elaborates,[46] but instead from an adjacent reflection on the role of groups per se. In her account, Scott situates this in the historical struggles of workers:

The idea that all individuals could be treated equally has inspired those who found themselves excluded from access to something they and their societies considered a right (education, work, subsistence wages, property, citizenship) to claim inclusion by challenging the standards upon which equality was granted to some and denied to others. Democratic-socialist workers demanding universal manhood suffrage in France in 1848 insisted 'that there will not be a citizen who can say to another "you are more sovereign than I"'.[47]

While this is a different argument, one can see how it might speak to the ways racial minorities as a group can continue to face discrimination at a group level today. In her discussion of the 'conundrum of equality', Scott sets out the challenges for fellow liberals in three stages:

1. Equality is an absolute principle and a historically contingent practice.
2. Group identities define individuals and deny the full expression or realization of their individuality.
3. Claims for equality involve the acceptance and rejection of the group identity attributed by discrimination. Or, to put it another way: the terms of exclusion on which discrimination is premised are at once refused and reproduced in demands for inclusion.[48]

What is being outlined here is a framing in which equality is meaningfully understood when placed within a proper historical and social context that takes into consideration the role and significance of groups. Scott elaborates:

> Group identities are an inevitable aspect of social and political life, and the two are interconnected because group differences become visible, salient and troubling in specific political contexts. It is at these moments – when exclusions are legitimated by group differences, when economic and social hierarchies advantage some groups at the expense of others, when one set of biological or religious or ethnic or cultural characteristics are valued over another – that the tension between individuals and groups emerges. Individuals for whom group identities were simply dimensions of a multi-faceted individuality, find themselves fully determined by a single element: religious or ethnic or racial or gender identity.[49]

These rationales are present in anti-discrimination measures that have proceeded through group-specific instruments to outlaw discrimination based not just on race and ethnicity, but also other identity groupings centring on gender, disability, age, sexual orientation and so forth, as well as sometimes insisting on the institutional monitoring of under-representation among such groups.[50] In terms of race and ethnicity in particular, public policies have included the *categorisation* of people and groups, for example on census forms or on ethnic monitoring forms, as well as addressing embedded disadvantage by actively prohibiting prejudicial behaviour, or promoting opportunity, or both. Being allegedly 'neutral' has also been an approach, typified by the non-discrimination promised in the French Constitution, which deems equal treatment *as uniformity* – a principle that functions to restate the racial status of the majority. Thus, the Constitution of the Fifth Republic (1958) promises to 'ensure the equality of all citizens before the law without distinction of origin, race or religion', when in practice it promotes the alleged cultural status of the White majority and racialises everything that deviates from this, particular French Muslims.[51]

This is in contrast to the kinds of affirmative action quotas and targets unevenly pursued in the US. What is notable is that affirmative action measures have developed in a way that places a specific emphasis on managing group relations, but which stops short of recognising the difference between sanctions required to tackle overt racism in society, and the wholesale reimagination required to tackle racist social systems. For Mills, this is not unconnected to a wider project of racial liberalism in which an 'idealizing white liberalism has bleached not merely the actual world but whited-out an objective perception of what would be required to right its wrongs'.[52]

At times, Britain has perhaps borrowed something from an American approach, but in a way that reaches beyond how minoritised groups might blend into society. This means that British anti-discrimination frameworks have, in places, tried to address the rights of distinct groups as well as their modes of interaction, and so are not merely concerned with the rights of individuals.[53] As such, from the legal response to racial discrimination in particular flows one characterisation of what is commonly known as 'British multiculturalism'.[54] This includes how, under the remit of national legislation, labour markets and other key arenas of British society have been host to contestations around equality of opportunity.

This includes recognising how ethnic and racial 'inequality rests on presumed differences [that] are not uniquely individualized, but taken to be categorical'.[55] The 'categorical' here refers to a named identity grouping, a move that is not unproblematic. It is often the case, for example, that too much emphasis is placed on internal strategies, hopes and aspirations, and too little on the external social context, such that we look for explanations in agency at the cost of looking to the social system as a whole. This is a hallmark of the Commission on Race and Ethnic Disparities (CRED), which insists that differential success in minority ethnic labour-market participation or educational outcomes is a function of culture where the role of ethnicity is 'mono-causal'.[56] Some, such as Kwame Anthony Appiah, have raised the related complaint that there is the risk that people become boxed into categories in ways that overlook heterogeneity:

> Demanding respect for people as blacks and as gays requires that there are some scripts that go with being an African-American or having same-sex desires. There will be proper ways of being black and gay, there will be expectations to be met, demands will be made. It is at this point that someone who takes autonomy seriously will ask whether we have not replaced one kind of tyranny with another.[57]

So, the concern here is that in trying to address a historical injustice, public policies that seek to take minority group categories into consideration *to address that historical disadvantage* begin to reify groups and essentialise their alleged properties. It is important to register that the precise criteria of groups are always contested, but might helpfully be configured according to boundaries that shift over time. To this end, Modood offers useful criteria *in addition* to identity, which include that of *disproportionality* in terms of the distribution of general negative societal characteristics such as unemployment, racial discrimination and poor health, among other inequalities.[58] The complaint nonetheless remains, that the ideational feedback to liberal theory remains impeded, because 'the non-transition over nearly half a century from ideal theory for well-ordered societies to non-ideal-theory-as-corrective-justice for what I have called "ill-ordered societies" ... is not accidental, not adventitious, but itself a manifestation of group privilege'.[59]

Another way in which some political theorists have understood these dynamics, at least in political theory, is to situate the same concerns in relation to prevailing debates between notions of recognition and redistribution. The latter is grounded in an egalitarian notion of justice which requires 'getting the privileged groups to share, by means of persuasion, pressure, or coercion, their resources with the poor and underprivileged'.[60] In this regard, redistribution 'primarily refers to the material resources which can be transferred from one group to another',[61] while recognition sees material resources as *interdependent* with those of status and identity. Redistribution has an old pedigree, Parekh reminds us, 'going back to the early Greek democrats, and includes influential Christian thinkers, millenarian movements Marxists and egalitarian liberals'.[62] It is therefore a core concern that has become intimately established between related questions of equality, while recognition is often seen as a more peripheral project. Some writers have tried to bring matters of equality together under the two registers; thus Nancy Fraser, in dialogue with Axel Honneth, eschews this dualism on the grounds that equality needs both redistribution and recognition to be aligned.[63]

To this end, Fraser introduces the category of a 'bivalent collectivity' to bring socioeconomic and cultural dimensions together. A bivalent collectivity includes groups that suffer both material maldistribution and cultural misrecognition, neither of which may be reduced to the other, because the injustice such a collectivity encounters emerges in both spheres. In Fraser's terms, 'People who are subject to both cultural injustice and economic injustice need both recognition and redistribution. They need both to claim and to deny their specificity.'[64] To overcome the redistribution–recognition dilemma, Fraser makes a distinction between two kinds of remedies for injustice, namely *affirmation* and *transformation*.[65] By affirmative remedies for injustice she means remedies aimed at correcting inequitable outcomes of social arrangements without disturbing the underlying framework that generates them. By transformative remedies, she is concerned with correcting inequitable outcomes precisely by restructuring the underlying frameworks.

While this is a valuable addition to overcoming the recognition–redistribution dualism, which partly emerges out of how redistribution has been configured in dominant theoretical traditions,[66] it insufficiently registers 'how no single language can adequately articulate the full range of diverse experiences of and insights into the structures of injustice'.[67] Hence the solution proposed by Fraser risks normatively narrowing the ways in which recognition and redistribution can be configured and related, creating a hierarchy of some harms over others and which, most obviously for our discussion, overlooks the role and function of institutional racism. This last point is more than about an individual author's contribution, of course, for it returns us to a discussion of how liberal scholarship assumes a kind of innocence for itself or, as Wang has argued, is produced from an assumption of being an honest broker, resting 'on the innocence of their location or subject position', one that refuses to entertain the lived realities of minoritised groups, 'allowing them peace of mind amidst the state of perpetual violence'.[68]

The 'clarion call' of institutional racism

It is a sentiment still felt more than 25 years since the racist murder of teenager Stephen Lawrence, which would eventually lead, after six years of campaigning, to a public inquiry deeming the UK's largest police authority guilty of institutional racism. As the inquiry report details, 17-year-old Stephen was repeatedly stabbed on his way home by a group of five or six young White men who shouted racist abuse before the attack. The inquiry documented the improper London Metropolitan Police Force investigation and the attendant findings, and the investigating judge found ample evidence of institutional racism across the organisation, defined in the following terms:

> For the purposes of our Inquiry the concept of institutional racism which we apply consists of:

> The collective failure of an organisation to provide an appropriate and professional service to people because of their colour, culture, or ethnic origin. It can be seen or detected in processes, attitudes and behaviour which amount to discrimination through unwitting prejudice, ignorance, thoughtlessness and racist stereotyping which disadvantage minority ethnic people.

> It persists because of the failure of the organisation openly and adequately to recognise and address its existence and causes by policy, example and leadership. Without recognition and action to eliminate such racism it can prevail as part of the ethos or culture of the organisation. It is a corrosive disease.[69]

The inquiry made a number of wide-ranging recommendations with a broad scope, which then had implications outside the police force in a manner that related to the public sector more broadly.[70] Then, much as now, a key issue relates to the role of what is deemed 'unwitting', a pivot point for how institutional racism came to be adjudicated in the inquiry. Convention is the key here, to the extent that individual motives and objectives become much less relevant to sustaining and proliferating racialised outcomes. This is important because a focus on social convention suggests that legislating against individual motives and objectives does not tackle how racial inequalities sustain and proliferate. Take the well-established but still shocking fact, highlighted in the *Black People, Racism and Human Rights* report in 2020, that while the rate of deaths of women in childbirth has fallen for White women (to 7 in 100,000), it has increased for Black women (to 38 in 100,000).[71] Quoted in the report, obstetrician and gynaecologist Dr Christine Ekechi describes how possible unwitting reasons operate when she says: 'People think of racism in an overt, aggressive way. But that's not always what it is. It's about biased assumptions – and we doctors have the same biases as anyone else.'[72] This might include attitudes among healthcare workers about Black patients having higher pain thresholds, being too demanding, or not understanding their treatment. For Black women in White spaces, these can prove lethal assumptions. They manifest in Black women not being listened to in health settings that are, in the final analysis, institutions, and so further illustrate what Ahmed describes as the function of 'institutional norms as somatic'.[73] By this she means that 'by assuming a body, institutions can generate an idea of appropriate conduct without making this explicit. The institute "institutes" the body that is instituting.'[74]

As the racial disproportionality of the COVID-19 pandemic further makes plain, and as discussed in the next chapter, although racial inequalities in health are driven by social and economic factors, harmful (and flawed) assumptions about 'culture' are pervasive and deflect responsibility onto the victims of systemic discrimination. For its part, the Macpherson Report was a very significant call for change, and its presentation by commissioners as a 'clarion call' was notable in their insistence that:

> the Stephen Lawrence Inquiry has provided such publicity and such awareness of the problems directly and indirectly revealed that there is now a signal opportunity to deal with specific matters arising from the murder and all that followed ... a clarion call to seize the chance to tackle and to deal with the general problems.[75]

What is so striking in these words is that they had been spoken before as well as after Stephen's murder. Formerly, in the Scarman Report, the chair specifically concluded that 'the evidence which I have received, the effect of which I have outlined ... leaves no doubt in my mind that racial disadvantage is a fact of current British life.... Urgent action is needed ...'.[76] Of course, unlike the Macpherson Report, the Scarman Inquiry was much more reticent to name institutional racism, and yet it could not deny 'that racialism and discrimination against black people – often hidden, sometimes unconscious – remain a major source of social tension and conflict'.[77] Outside of policing narrowly conceived, the definition would later resonate in the Home Office and its treatment of the Windrush Generation.

The *Windrush Lessons Learned Review* (2020), conducted by Wendy Williams, offered the following assessment:

> While I am unable to make a definitive finding of institutional racism within the department, I have serious concerns that these failings demonstrate an institutional ignorance and thoughtlessness towards the issue of race and the history of the Windrush generation within the department, which are consistent with some elements of the definition of institutional racism.[78]

The characterisations of 'social tension' and conflict in Scarman, and 'institutional ignorance' in Williams, are apolitical ways of describing what has unfolded, underwritten by the systemic racism theorised in Chapter One and documented earlier in this chapter, but obscured through the disavowal of race in identity discussed in Chapter Two. None of this masks the visceral character of continuing racial encounters with the state, and institutional racism within the ranks of the Metropolitan Police Service, that continue to this day, as captured in the experience of a young Black woman 27 years after the murder of Stephen Lawrence:

> Having a male officer using all his body weight, burying his knee into my neck and using all the power within him to try to cut off my air supply … I just remember things turning like they looked a bit radioactive to me because… I was losing consciousness.… I was pinned down again, I'll say about five, six, seven officers. I couldn't breathe. I kept begging them to stop. It was the same officer that was punching me outside the restaurant who still went on to punch me while I was fully unclothed.[79]

Knowledge of such ongoing cases was perhaps why Baroness Doreen Lawrence asked the joint committee, 'How many more lessons do we all need to learn? The lessons are there already for us to implement'.[80] Perhaps one answer then rests in enforcement. It is notable that the joint committee specifically states that 'the Equality and Human Rights Commission (EHRC) has been unable to adequately provide leadership and gain trust in tackling racial inequality in the protection and promotion of human rights'.[81] It is an observation that confirms a widely held view among community groups. That an amalgamated equality body ran the risk of both diluting and de-prioritising race equality was a frequently aired concern when the EHRC was first created in 2007,[82] bringing all the existing equality 'grounds' (race, gender, disability) together before assuming responsibility for newer ones (age, sexual orientation, and religion or belief) in anticipation of the Equality Act 2010. That these precise concerns have come to pass surprises nobody outside of an organisation that few race equality stakeholders feel connected to, something typified by its nearly all-White board of commissioners. That it has not one Black commissioner is a disgrace, and is itself evidence of a profound institutional failure on race equality. Ultimately, it is the cruellest example of what the Stephen Lawrence Inquiry envisioned, especially when it insisted that:

> There must be an unequivocal acceptance of the problem of institutional racism and its nature before it can be addressed, as it needs to be, in full partnership with members of minority ethnic communities. There is no doubt that recognition, acknowledgement and acceptance of the problem by Police Services and their officers is an important first step for minority ethnic communities in moving forward positively to solve the problem which exists.[83]

The disparities that are found in the labour market, higher education and housing sectors reappear in areas such as formal and informal school exclusions and criminal justice where, in England, Black children are nearly three times more likely to be permanently excluded than White British pupils.[84] Indeed, *Black People, Racism and Human Rights* showed only that school exclusions are not unconnected to rates of incarceration, and that 'in the last decade, the extent to which black children and young people are disproportionately targeted by the youth justice system has increased'.[85] This claim is further demonstrated by consulting youth justice statistics for 2018/19 in England and Wales, which show that Black children (who make up about 4 per cent of the entire population aged between 10 and 17 years) are four times more likely to be arrested than their White counterparts, and nearly three times more likely to receive a caution or custodial sentence. In 2018/19 the percentage of Black children in custody had significantly increased to 28 per cent of the entire population held in youth custody (compared with 15 per cent a decade ago). In each instance, and as Sewell has argued, translation of race as an 'abstract idea of race into a concrete social fact' is necessary not on premeditated design, but in the prevailing attitudes, values and beliefs.[86]

'Pessimistic narratives'

How, then, can something so morally unjust sit comfortably as normalised social outcomes in Britain, despite successive governments wielding the means to address it? This is at heart the question that motivates researchers, activists and minoritised groups who continually identify the drivers of racial inequalities, and who are long accustomed with the obfuscations that stymie change. Smith, Allen and Danley have characterised something of these dynamics as 'racial battle fatigue',[87] and while the concept typically focuses more on interpersonal encounters, it nonetheless resonates in how our work on these topics was described in the recently published report by the Commission on Race and Ethnic Disparities (CRED) as an 'example of overly pessimistic narratives'.[88] While much of the report might have been predicted, few of us nonetheless anticipated the Commission would seek to make a virtue of racial inequalities by presenting them 'as a beacon to the rest of Europe and the world'.[89] In what the Commission was persuaded is an uplifting account, its report seeks to pivot from the required focus on social systems, structures and institutions to – as we are told from the outset – 'the other reasons for minority success and failure, including those embedded in the cultures and attitudes of those minority communities themselves'.[90]

It does not require a trained eye to appreciate that ignoring a problem in order not to see it is methodologically unsound, yet this is an orientation long associated with the Commission's chair, Tony Sewell, who has previously insisted that Black British African Caribbean children fare less well in schools not because of their treatment, since 'even when faced with white racism, these black students are their own worst enemies'.[91] Scaled up to the UK level (though largely focusing on England), and stretched across a variety of sectors beyond education, the Commission adopted an expanded version of this 'cultural deficit' view, but added to it the purported role of compounding factors. Specifically, the report insisted that racial inequality should be viewed a second order effect that cannot be uncoupled from class, geography, employment or education. Both rationales inform the Commission's stated ambition to move away from a discussion of institutional racism, and instead 'look elsewhere for the roots of that disadvantage'.[92] Neither of these objectives bear scrutiny, as illustrated in the responses to the public call for evidence which overwhelming show the contrary.[93]

As a government-endorsed Commission, it was the worst in a generation, and failed to grasp the key features of more than 50 years of evidence that such research typically builds on in favour of anecdotes which further drive attention away from systemic explanatory variables. As such, it is telling how the Commission's view, that it 'is possible to have racial disadvantage without racists',[94] unintentionally repeats the title of a highly critical and landmark text by Bonilla-Silva. In this, the author explains how it is *precisely* the logic adopted by the Commission that sustains and proliferates racial inequality, and is itself 'a distillate of racial ideology and, hence, of white supremacy'.[95] While striking to note, it is not surprising, given none of the commissioners has any recognised research competence in the study of racism, while the few qualified academics named in the report say they were not properly consulted,[96] and illustrates how an alleged post-racial politics 'is a powerful force, and rewards those that seem to carry its promise'.[97] Refusing to build on the collective insights before it, the report ultimately is uncoupled from the experience of those it purports to focus on and is, moreover, invidious in adopting a type of approach that Cho has previously characterised as 'political retreat from race by redefining the terms for racial politics', and where '[n]ot only are racial remedies and racial discourse off the table, but so are acts of collective political organization and resistance by racialized individuals'.[98] Perhaps in the final analysis that was its purpose, as Baroness Doreen Lawrence put it: to push 'the fight against racism back 20 years or more'.[99] As researchers, and however much racial battle fatigue this may bring, it is not a fight any of us should ignore, and we should instead reorient our focus to Bowling's submission to the Stephen Lawrence Inquiry and, specifically, his description of how '[i]nstitutional racism affects the routine ways in which ethnic minorities are treated in their capacity as employees, witnesses, victims, suspects and members of the general public'.[100] As the racial disproportionality highlighted by the COVID-19 pandemic makes plain, we can once more see this in how racial inequalities in health are driven by social and economic factors, where harmful (and flawed) assumptions are pervasive, and which too often deflect from the role of social systems.

FOUR

The racial realities of COVID-19

How can we explain the disproportionalities made so starkly visible by the COVID-19 pandemic, and why have authorities been so reticent to recognise the ways in which racism heightens vulnerability for minoritised groups at all levels of society? Certainly, health inequalities policies in different countries have looked at deprivation and socioeconomic inequalities,[1] but the impact of COVID-19 made it clear, once more, that racial inequality also needs to be a distinct focus. Simply put, the accumulated evidence has made it harder to deny outright that 'intersections between socioeconomic status, ethnicity and racism intensify inequalities in health for ethnic groups'.[2] Harder to deny and unwilling to deny are not, of course, the same thing. For example, the appeal to explanations of pre-existing conditions to explain COVID-19-related disparities remain frequent. Yet these inequalities are themselves temporal and reflect the distribution of income, labour market sectors and work patterns, residential location and overcrowded accommodations.[3] The key point that remains valid across health and racial disparities, as Phelan and Link observed, is that ignoring racism as a direct driver misattributes a fundamental cause of health inequalities, something apparent in the ongoing impact of the pandemic, including the roll-out and take-up of vaccinations.[4] This chapter will explore this as a continuing issue that has moved beyond the early stages of the pandemic, in order to show why it is essential for societies to focus on the racial determinants of health, in ways that are different from prevailing approaches pursued up to now, in grasping something of how 'diseases that disproportionately impact people of color are tied to long histories of exploitation, dispossession, and devaluation of the lives of Black, Indigenous, and other people of color'.[5]

All in it together?

A prevailing feature of the political rhetoric throughout the COVID-19 pandemic was to characterise it as a common and shared experience. A closer examination of its impact, however, quickly reveals something very different. By the time the UK was officially experiencing the 'second wave', in late 2020, and thereafter a second lockdown, the racial disproportionalities once more revealed the ways in which 'structural injustice cuts short the lives of people subjected to systemic racism and economic deprivation'.[6] In England, Public Health England (PHE) reported that Black men were four times, and Asian men three times, more likely to die of COVID-19 than their White British male counterparts.[7] Black women, meanwhile, were almost three times, and Asian women two and a half times, more likely to die than White British women. In Scotland, the rates compared to White Scottish groups were estimated to be around threefold higher in Pakistani and Mixed groups, and around twofold higher in Indian and Other Asian groups. This disproportionate outcome mirrors a picture that has emerged elsewhere, including in the United States, Sweden and Spain.[8]

Perhaps seeking to render 'invisible the racial sinews of the body politic and modes of rule and regulation',[9] the only time the UK government broached the role of systemic racism as a contributing factor was in order to deny it. Instead, and borrowing from Ray's study of social organisations,[10] we might say that the disproportionality described earlier and in what follows has frequently relied on a 'naturalization of racial categories, and their subsequent legitimation', such that it is no surprise biological explanations, rather than systemic ones, are still promoted to account for disparities. Hence, one researcher publishing in the *British Medical Journal*, for example, suggested that 'BAME individuals ... lack knowledge on the importance of a balanced and healthy diet containing all essential micronutrients that are required to boost immunity and prevent infectious diseases'.[11] This is what we might call a lifestyle behaviour/biological explanation. It is easier to refute than the explanations attributing the disproportionate burden of COVID-19 on ethnic and racial minorities to greater levels of pre-existing chronic health conditions in these groups, for these are necessarily part of an explanation. Indeed, at the most proximal level, greater levels of pre-existing chronic health conditions, such as cardiovascular disease, hypertension and diabetes, which are the most common comorbidities observed in COVID-19 fatalities,[12] are indeed apparent among Black and minority ethnic groups.[13] The explanatory role these play, however, comes into view only when set in a wider context which reveals their social and political causes, and not solely their clinical ones. For example, and as noted in the previous chapter, Black and minority ethnic groups tend to have poorer socioeconomic circumstances, something long connected to poorer health outcomes, and which is further compounded by being more likely to live in overcrowded accommodation, increasing risk of transmission within households. Once infected, many of the pre-existing health conditions that increase the risk of having severe infection are more common in Black and minority ethnic groups.[14]

The significance of these explanations is perhaps the best example of a multi-temporal concern, precisely because medicine has been a crucible in race making, especially by supporting the idea of valid underlying biological differences between human populations. For the *key point*, which cannot be overstated, is that these comorbidities make minority ethnic populations more susceptible to critical complications if they contract COVID-19, not because ethnic and racial categories are themselves a causal factor, but because they map onto underlying social determinants which generate these conditions. This argument is supported by how these conditions are not only more prevalent in many UK minority ethnic groups than in the ethnic majority but are also manifest at an earlier age of onset. For example, a striking finding from the Health Survey for England is that the health of White English people aged 61–70 is comparable to that of Caribbean and Indian people aged 46–50, Pakistani people aged 36–40 and Bangladeshi people aged 26–30.[15] Another way of stating this is to say that the higher levels of chronic ill health manifest among racialised minority groups are to a considerable extent the product of an inequality that itself is a legacy of racial discrimination from the earliest stages of the migration process, when newly arrived Citizens of the United Kingdom and Colonies began to be incorporated into the lowest rungs of the UK's segmented labour market. This is precisely what was meant in the previous chapter by the discussion of the long tail of racial discrimination, insofar as it continues to play a key role in predisposing minority ethnic groups to chronic ill health.[16] This includes the pervasive effects of institutional racism whereby policies 'unwittingly' sanction the 'production and exploitation of group-differentiated vulnerability to premature death'.[17]

Centring the social determinants

Let us then re-centre what we call the 'social determinants' of health. By this is meant the need to maintain a broad focus on the underlying determinants of susceptibility to the virus and not allow the physiological risks to be separated from their social exposures. It demands that we take both a historical view and also a more conceptually discerning approach to seemingly self-evident data and its use in public health and policy responses.[18] This begins by appreciating something of the longstanding relationship between medical knowledge and race, which has developed into a broader account about how we think of health and well-being, and the kinds of differential outcomes that we routinely see. For example, it is sometimes said the genetic condition of sickle cell anaemia is a predominantly 'Black disease',[19] which suggests that a discrete relationship exists between a racial category and biology. Or, it is observed, that because there are higher levels of hypertension among African Americans when compared with White Americans,[20] a physiological explanation emerging from the group category is self-evident. A further illustration might be elevated levels of psychosis and poorer mental health among some minority ethnic and racial groups, something reflected in the over-representation of members of these minoritised groups in mental health institutions.[21]

If we take each example in turn, we can see why we must wholly reject attributions of a causal relation between ethnic and racial categories and disease uncoupled from their social exposures, and instead be willing to be guided by an understanding of the sociological conditions in the environment that frame such conditions. Beginning with sickle cell anaemia, it is clear that this condition results from genetic alteration in levels of haemoglobin protein in the red blood cells, which become brittle and sickle-shaped. Yet, on inspection, we find that it correlates with a legacy of exposure to a particular kind of malaria (falciparum), to which people with sickle cell anaemia are actually more resistant. Since malaria is (or has been) a significant cause of death across continents, from West Africa to the Mediterranean coastline, as well as in India, we can observe a historical gene–environment interaction – or a 'selection pressure' (environmental factors influencing' the process of natural selection) – which continues to carry this sickle cell gene even though it is sometimes harmful.[22] As a consequence, we find cases of sickle cell anaemia among a wider variety of population groups than may commonly be anticipated, including White groups.

Turning to higher levels of hypertension, an important relationship between social stigma and anxiety that affects hypertension is illustrated in a study by Gravlee,[23] who makes a useful distinction between cultural and biological dimensions of skin colour in Puerto Rico. He does so in order to explore the relationship between biological and environmental indicators of race by first studying local ways of talking about skin colour and how skin colour shapes Puerto Ricans' exposure to racism and other social stresses. To measure this, he developed a survey to compare blood pressure to the significance of colour, as local people understood colour. Strikingly, what he found has wide-ranging implications, because he was able to show that darker-skinned people were associated with higher blood pressure, in a way that supports the thesis that the social aspects of race, such as stigma and discrimination, can also have biological consequences – precisely, an inversion of what is often presumed to be the case. Indeed, and in an earlier study taking a life-course approach to the same topic, Geronimus introduced the idea of 'weathering'.[24] In his study it was found that Black Americans experience a marked deterioration in their health because of the accumulated social stresses that come with being a racial minority in a society that deems their value to be of negative worth. This has been taken up in the work of McEwen, among others, who advanced the idea of 'allostatic load' to describe 'the cumulative wear and tear on the body's systems owing to repeated adaptation stressors'.[25]

What Gravlee, Geronimus and McEwen point to is that the experience, perception or anticipation of discrimination can increase levels of individual and social stress and anxiety.[26] The important observation is that differences in social and cultural environments between groups mean that different physiological outcomes will emerge, something that takes us to our last example: elevated levels of psychosis and poorer mental health among some ethnic and racial minority groups, as reflected in the over-representation of members of these groups in mental health institutions.[27] What is interesting is that while African Caribbean groups in Britain are three to five times more likely to be diagnosed with severe mental health problems (and much more likely to be admitted for schizophrenia), they are much less likely to be diagnosed with neurosis. As Sharply established, 'many of the factors suggested are associated, in the general population, with an increased risk of nonpsychotic disorders such as depression, anxiety and functional somatic symptoms rather than psychotic disorders'.[28]

It has long been known that Black groups appear much less likely to receive a diagnosis of anxiety or depression from their general practitioner than non-Black attenders.[29] Yet the same groups tend to be over-represented in a number of secure institutions, including hospitals, prisons and medium secure units. So, in terms of incidence – when these groups come into contact with formal agencies (rather than wider prevalence at large) – they fare significantly less well than other groups.[30] In this respect and more, argue Karlsen and Nazroo, 'the effects of racism on social identity, social status and economic position are also often ignored'.[31]

Re-centring race

So, prior to the onset of the pandemic, it had long been established that minority ethnic and racial groups systemically experience poorer health outcomes than many of their majority group counterparts. This should not imply, as Chaturvedi argues, that research which emphasises high rates of disease in minority ethnic groups indicates that ethnicity is the driver of these disparities.[32] What it instead shows are the serious concerns about the ways in which the concepts of ethnicity and race are discussed and measured within health research. A material illustration of this comes in Braun's account of the use of the spirometer, an instrument evaluating lung capacity, through which Black ethnic groups in the US are typically characterised as lacking 'vital capacity', and so are less likely to be medically insured for what are deemed inherent characteristics.[33] Some researchers believe the complexity of ethnicity and of its relationship to socioeconomic position may, in the end, render it of limited use in studying health inequalities[34] and, specifically, that the features of explanation attributed to ethnicity are in fact a façade for accumulated material inequality due in no small part to racism. In similar terms, Karlsen and Nazroo elaborate the ways in which key contributory features cannot be divorced from one another:

> [A]spects of the relationship between ethnicity, social position and health are generally ignored in empirical health research. In particular, measures of social position often fail to account for the accumulation of disadvantage over the life-course – measuring socio-economic status only at one-time point – and they typically ignore the role of ecological effects resulting from the concentration of ethnic minority groups in particular residential areas.[35]

What is being argued, therefore, is that we must guard against explanations of some real inherent ethnic factor and insist remain vigilant of mono-causal explanations. Rejecting the explanation of ethnicity alone, however, is not the same as rejecting ethnicity per se. For despite the difficulties in defining and measuring a concept as complex as ethnicity, it is no more challenging than measuring socioeconomic position or social class and, furthermore, understanding ethnic and racial variations is crucial to determining the role of different exposures to disease risk, as well as providing important information for the targeting of public health interventions and resources.[36] These various concerns and debates are only likely to be resolved with greater reflection on measuring and constructing both ethnicity and socioeconomic positions.[37] The key point is that from a Social Determinant of Health perspective, we must resist the ways in which ethnicity is pressed in to service the appeal 'of racial-genetic determinism',[38] which overlooks systemic explanations for higher levels of chronic illness and their relationship to social stresses – including direct and indirect racial discrimination.

That last point is important because we should ask why we would expect disparities in health outcomes to be different from the disparities in education, criminal justice system or child welfare. This requires us to return to the framing and evidence of earlier chapters to use concepts and categories that hold an explanatory function in other arenas of social life, and where racial injustice is almost in 'the design of things' and 'the design of relationships'.[39] These are precisely the ancillary spheres that require a systemic approach to bring into view as part of a whole. As Chapter Three established, we know that racism plays a profound role in lower incomes, lower status occupations, poorer employment conditions, worse educational outcomes – all of which shape health outcomes. Ultimately these are the key concerns if we want to think seriously about disproportionate impact of the pandemic, and specifically to critically interrogate the idea that we are all in it together. It is for these reasons, and 'while also pointing to our common humanity', that COVID-19 'has pulled the thread, revealing profound inequities in every country it touches'.[40] In other words, these inequalities are not an avatar of wider inequalities but instead, as Phelan and Link argue from the US perspective, 'the connection between race and health outcomes endures largely because racism is a fundamental cause of racial differences in SES [social economic status] and because SES is a fundamental cause of health inequalities'.[41] That is to say, racial discrimination continues to play a key role in predisposing minority ethnic groups to chronic ill health.[42] This includes the pervasive effects of institutional racism whereby policies 'unwittingly' permit White people to gain more from education, the labour market and health systems – as is reflected in the marginal attention given to the racial–ethnic dimensions of health inequality in policy responses.[43] In the UK, COVID-19 and the government's response to it have the potential to amplify the existing socioeconomic disparities and racial discrimination that undergird ethnic health inequalities. For the same factors that predispose people from minority ethnic groups to live and work in circumstances that engender chronic ill health are those that will make it harder for people from those groups to protect themselves from COVID-19 through social distancing.[44]

These factors include how workers from minority racial groups have moved into private sector work in the service industries on the one hand (an issue we return to later) and into public sector employment on the other.[45] In particular, non-White groups are hugely over-represented among NHS staff who, as keyworkers, have continued to go to their workplaces, where they face exposure to the virus. As the Lawrence Review notes, while making up around 14 per cent in the general population, Black and minority ethnic staff constitute about 20 per cent of the entire NHS workforce, a figure that increases to 44 per cent of medical staff.[46] This was especially apparent in the early incidents of deaths in health workers and led Dr Chaand Nagpaul, as Chair of the British Medical Association, to call for a review into the disproportionate numbers of deaths among doctors from minority ethnic backgrounds.[47] Moreover, evidence shows that there are higher levels of COVID-19 infection and related deaths for racial minorities in healthcare settings.[48] This excess mortality among non-White health staff certainly reflects the concentration of minority ethnic staff in healthcare roles within the NHS, and aligns with the General Medical Council and British Medical Association's prior findings concerning Black and minority ethnic doctors' reluctance to complain about workplace safety.[49] All of which, of course, compounds, rather than displaces the existing ethnic and racial inequalities in health sectors. It is especially pernicious that healthcare workers are placed under pressure in unsafe work, not least in accepting working in risky situations.[50]

What is true of healthcare workers is true of the wider population, where ethnic and racial minorities have been incorporated into the UK's segmented labour market in ways that direct them predominantly towards sectors offering few job protections, including provisions for sick leave and sick pay.[51] Compared with White British workers, minority ethnic workers are more likely to be on agency contracts or zero-hours contracts, and more likely to be in temporary work.[52] As Liebman et al put it, 'the spectacular cruelty that the COVID-19 pandemic illuminates is not new, highlighting bio- and necropolitical capitalist landscapes long in the making. Yet the virus exposes how these dynamics are constantly in flux as capital struggles to reproduce itself and makes unstable alliances with the State'.[53] We know, for example, that larger percentages of some minority ethnic groups, notably Pakistani men, are self-employed and thus were likely to forgo income during the lockdowns.[54] From the gender disaggregated data, minority ethnic women, particularly Black African and Caribbean women, are over-represented in social care work.[55] Most ethnic minorities, particularly Pakistani, Bangladeshi and Black African groups, have significantly lower earnings, are more likely to be paid below the statutory minimum[56] and are already in financial poverty. Similarly, Pakistani and Bangladeshi workers are especially likely to be employed in the distribution and transport sectors, where as key workers they are obliged to remain at work and risk personal exposure.[57] In these contexts, it is arguable that 'the discourse of the "essential worker" is inseparable from racialized essentialism that deems some bodies naturally disposed to risk and premature death. While workers are applauded "for their 'sacrifices', they are actually being sacrificed"'.[58]

If ever there was a need to be vigilant about the attribution of causal relations between ethnic and racial categories and disease, COVID-19 provides it. 'The science of race', Washington reminds us, 'has always been an amalgam of logic and culture'. A sociological understanding of the conditions in the environment that frame and register this science of race is the only way we can ensure policy makers at least entertain the underlying determinants of susceptibility to the virus, and do not uncouple these from their social determinants.[59] Presently, the effects of racism on health outcomes is insufficiently understood because there is an unwillingness to grasp how experiences of racial discrimination are linked to numerous mental and physical health outcomes, including asthma and hypertension, and that these processes do not operate in isolation: they co-occur and sequentially lead to deepening inequalities in many domains across a person's lifecourse, and might be transmitted from one generation to the next. It is very rare to hear concepts such as that of 'weathering' the 'life-course' with regards to race in government circles. Specifically, the long-term impact of the compounding effect of discrimination and social stress, which is documented to lower immune responses, remains overlooked.[60] The present difficulty is apparent in an overwhelming inability to grasp differences in occupational exposures, income and housing conditions, and differential vulnerabilities in underlying health conditions and comorbidities, as well as differential access to treatment and other forms of support. This is acutely apparent for people seeking asylum, who continue to face racialised barriers often to access the most basic health services, in line with a wider experience of racialisation to which we turn next.

FIVE

(De-)racialising refuge

This chapter focuses on what in disciplinary terms is often seen as an adjacent concern to that of racial justice, namely the topic of migration and issues of asylum and refuge in particular. Often, the distinctions between the categories of 'migrant', 'asylum seeker' and 'refugee' are artefactual and give insufficient attention to the processes whereby these groups are constructed. A focus on asylum and refuge, and the fluidity between these categories and race, reminds us of Du Bois's observation that '[p]erhaps it is wrong to speak of it [race] at all as a "concept" rather than as a group of contradictory forces, facts, and tendencies'.[1] This includes how the distinctions between these categories are used to reproduce notions of deserving and undeserving lives, in ways similar to those Agamben characterised as being caught in a 'zone of indistinction' (reduced to 'bare life' and all the curtailment to life this may bring).[2] Certainly, it is hard to disagree with De Genova that:

> anyone concerned with questions of race and racism today must readily recognize that they present themselves in a particularly acute way in the European migration context, haunted as Europe's borders are by an appalling proliferation of almost exclusively non-European/non-white migrant and refugee deaths and other forms of structural violence and generalized suffering.[3]

There is, of course, a longstanding literature that has connected these concerns, including works by Goldberg, who has been especially influential in this regard, arguing that nation-states are also racial states in their organisation of citizenship, notions of belonging and access to the polity more broadly.[4] The appeal of this framing is especially found in ethical tendencies, particularly those that allow us to understand how states can maintain as self-evident that 'certain human lives are more grievable than others'.[5] For Goldberg, these tendencies are underwritten by what he identifies as the two traditions of the racial state – *naturalism* and *historicism*: each tradition presents border controls as necessary measures to 'preserve' the racial integrity of European nation-states.[6] It takes nothing from the force of this argument to pivot to a focus on cities, and to track social formations that, on one level, seek to refuse the racial state, for what this allows us to see, through a different literature, is how social systems are not monolithic. This analysis could not be more relevant.

According to the International Organization for Migration (IOM), over 1.6 million displaced migrants and refugees entered Europe in 2015 at the height of the so-called refugee crisis.[7] By the middle of 2020, COVID-19 largely brought the movement of people to a halt as individual states and whole regional blocs introduced travel restrictions.[8] Much happened in between these points, and this chapter looks for optimism in a number of prevailing tendencies in order to consider what may be learned from shifting our gaze from the national to the local, specifically to ask if it is possible to de-racialise refuge through rescaling solidarities from the nation-state to the city. This is not to ignore the multi-temporal character of our racial present, to encourage a kind of 'discretionary humanitarianism',[9] nor to sanitise European cities as saviours. It is instead a sociological consideration of social relations, and the political possibilities these might herald; specifically, how the pervasiveness of an 'ostensible exclusion, in which the purported naturalness and putative necessity of exclusion' might be challenged, and where the death of people seeking refuge could be more than regrettable.

We might begin with the story of Domenico Lucano, noting how it must be a strange predicament to be banished from the town of which you were the mayor. So became the status of

Lucano, a once local teacher and then mayor of Riace in the south of Italy.[10] Mimmo, as he became known to the people of Riace, met the full force of the anti-immigrant politics of Matteo Salvini and the Lega party in 2018, then in coalition government, while Salvini served as interior minister. The underlying reason? The town of which Mimmo was mayor led pioneering schemes from the early 2000s to incorporate displaced migrants and refugees. His mayoralty founded an association, City of the Future (inspired by the Calabrian utopianist Tommaso Campanella), and secured some modest funding which allowed them to successfully incorporate people seeking refuge into local labour markets, and in ways that regenerated not only previously abandoned quarters, but the very sociality of Riace itself. As such, the city staked a claim for reimagining the space in ways that did not marginalise displaced migrants and refugees – precisely what the writer Lefebvre characterised both as the abstract claim to city life and as a concrete claim to spaces of work, leisure, education, healthcare and accommodation that should be shared by all urban dwellers.[11]

It is important not to romanticise this example or brush over its flaws, but instead to highlight that even though people may not have had a formal legal status, they nonetheless had a right to the city. For notably, and in addition to national policy and politics, the Riace model was also explicitly set against the Calabrian Mafia, who continue today to exploit migrants and refugees, in agricultural labour, in particular, where 12-hour shifts picking fruit in 40-degree heat is normal life, and which, with other coercion and violence, provides a case study of modern-day slavery in the European Union.

The 'Riace model', as it became known, was exported to other nearby towns and cities in the South of Italy[12] (as discussed later), and so is related to other examples of city and local-level governance that has operated within national-level racialised closure to refuge. The International Cities of Refuge Network, Cities of Sanctuary, the Save Me Campaign and the Eurocities network are illustrative of the ways that might signal a re-crafting of social imaginaries that elevates the capacity of cities 'to foster new forms of solidarity'.[13] Our enthusiasm for the study of these developments, however, should not overlook how cities are also sites in which national racial exclusions are enacted and realised locally, or, in other words, the ways in which systems prevail. This leans against a kind of methodological localism that can downplay 'situations of interdependence',[14] through which racial boundaries are forged and reapplied. Another way of putting this, borrowing from Stone,[15] is that, at the city level as much as the national level, the 'processes of becoming a refugee, of migration, of admission to a new country and of trying to build a new life, are all interwoven with the histories of nation-states'. Perhaps, however, this repeats precisely the error cautioned against in the opening chapter, namely approaches that foreclose agency, minimise resistance, and collapse the 'refusal' of racial minorities into mere objects of racist social systems.

Cities of hope?

To start elsewhere, we might turn to a discussion contained in a working paper by the late Zygmunt Bauman, who began to develop an account of what he termed 'cities of fears, and cities of hopes'.[16] It is a cliché, of course, to say cities are places where strangers meet, and yet in this, for Bauman, are the *fears* of change, and the *hopes*, conversely, of what change might bring. Both, he argued, are related to the same impulse, and reflect how the '[c]ity and social change are almost synonymous. Change is the quality of city life and the mode of urban existence. Change and city may, and indeed should, be defined by reference to each other'.[17] As is perhaps true of a good deal of his later work, Bauman was openly reflecting on a longstanding and weighty literature on the study of cities, of which he too was a student, and which, curiously, he did not revisit in his subsequent description of the 'refugee crisis' as 'humanity's crisis'.[18] The literature on cities meanwhile spans disciplines and methodologies, scales of the micro, meso and macro, questions of agency and structure, and matters of capital and community. Any historical account of this literature would include Max Weber's typology of 'city-generating factors',[19] which came partly in a rejection of Georg Simmel's characterisation of the city as a contingent outcome of its cumulative size and the scale of corresponding social relations – one feature of Simmel's broader account that is a flagstone of Kingsley Davis's later formulation of urbanisation as the expansion of a city's population in relation to the total national size.[20] It is with new dynamics of urbanism that both Simmel and Weber were grappling but, for Weber, 'size alone, certainly, cannot be decisive'.[21]

To build an ideal type for the present, and not untypically, Weber looked backwards to the medieval guilds that combined economic enterprise and religious activity as well as private and public life – something in which community progressively deteriorates with the onset of capitalism. Weber's typology of the city as spanning markets, social relations and bureaucracies continues to be of sociological purchase,[22] and with some clumsy discomfort, in each mode we can locate important examples over the last 30 years. For example, on markets, Saskia Sassen's *Global City* has probably been among the most influential of contemporary discussions, in which global cities are studied as financial market-centres and as sites where the command structures of global capital are geographically decentralised but not devolved.[23] Taking London specifically, Doreen Massey elaborated this through her focus on the deregulation, financialisation and commercialisation of all aspects of life that result in an ever more unequal world.[24]

Missing from these accounts is what Glick Schiller tracks as 'the transformation of human bodies into a commodity to be bought, trafficked or stored by multi-scalar agencies, including detention centres [that are] part of a process of accumulation through dispossession'.[25] These too are among the hallmarks of the development of urban space in neoliberal terms, which includes a double displacement of marginalised groups and their replacement with economically mobile populations with greater consumer potential. In particular, regeneration processes can rely on constructions of asylum seekers and refugees to 'pathologise' targeted locations with racialised and class-based discourses which attach a 'territorial stigma' to both people and place.[26] It is in this mode that we need to locate Panglossian statements about the capacity of cities presented in places such as Barber's popular tract *If Mayors Ruled the World*.[27] This is one unfortunate reading of the administrative and legal capacity of cities, for it misconceives how refugee services and infrastructure are delivered not by cities but by multinational businesses.

Of the role of social dwellings within Weber's typology, we might turn to the literature on the everyday, including Back and Sinha's *Migrant City*[28] and Suzanne Hall's study of a single road in South London whose residents showed the transnational character and points of departure which spanned the former British Empire.[29] The point is that migration in all its variety is a city-generating factor and should be understood as such. How, and in what ways, varies. The historical growth and expansion of cities, as well as their role and function in processes development, has conditioned the production and direction of migratory flows. At the same time, migration and migrants themselves continually (re)shape the city and urban life, and so contribute to the wider processes of change cherished by Bauman. Yet all of this is necessarily subject to the character of specific cities. Kloosterman makes this point in his discussion of 'cognitive cultural urban landscapes' – how specific cities lend themselves to types of opportunity structures for migrant entrepreneurship.[30] From a very different perspective, Albertsen and Diken's discussion of port cities offers another perspective, focusing on the relationship between low-income casual labour and migration, and how this has been central in forging 'welfare cities'.[31]

Governing 'home'

Having established these relationships, we can now slightly pivot our focus to observe not only how the city is often a means of grasping at migration, or vice versa, but also how both the literature on the city and the literature on migrant negotiations of it downplay the role of governance – especially the governance of displaced migrants and refugees. This deserves much more attention. It is where Bauman's notion of 'cities of fears' and 'cities of hopes' is most stark; something that traverses not only the 'everyday' but also supposedly high-level policy concerns. For it is in policy governance no less than in the multiculture of urban life that the boundaries of city life are forged. This includes how city governance seeks to racialise and deter displaced migration rather than facilitate entry, let alone pursue various strategies for 'integration'.

These are important concerns because in the emergent modes of governance that have accompanied the so-called migration crisis, the local and city-level articulations of migrant and refugee reception have had to negotiate national-level policy and rhetoric.[32] One feature of this is how local and city-level approaches especially rely on associations from the third sector, which have assumed a key role in what Elia has termed 'bottom up welfare'.[33] To what extent these local approaches offset the racialised national discourse and policy is therefore important, and asking this question through a focus on the key issue of housing is revealing for a number of reasons. Firstly, an interest in housing and settlement is as old as the study of race and the city, and some of the early features of this work continue to structure prevailing assumptions – such as, for example, the Chicago School's premise that spatial distance is a measure of social distance. In addition, while there is an emerging literature addressing the housing and accommodation trajectories of displaced migration and refugees, it is often material that is single case focused and ethnographically driven – both of which are assets in understanding the migration–asylum nexus. Less well established, however, are multi-case and multi-scalar policy governance accounts charting contemporary developments.

To explore this, in the next part of the chapter we reflect on developments in a number of medium-sized European cities known for leaning against national-level policy and rhetoric: Glasgow, Malmö and Cosenza. These are broadly comparable in terms of their size but their migration histories differ considerably. Recent displaced migrants have been accommodated, for example, in Glasgow since the mid-twentieth century; however, in the main, this was achieved through managed refugee resettlement programmes, which brought small numbers of recognised refugee groups to Scotland. This changed significantly with the then Labour UK government's dispersal scheme, which was intended to 'share' the accommodation of asylum seekers across the UK (principally shifting populations in the south east of England). To date, Glasgow is the only local authority in Scotland to have participated in the dispersal scheme, and is estimated to accommodate up to 2,000 asylum seekers annually, the largest intake for a single local authority in the UK. Malmö, meanwhile, is in the Scania province of Sweden, situated in Öresund region that connects Sweden to Denmark and the European continent. Malmö is the third largest city in Sweden, located on the border with Denmark, and bears a longstanding migration history. In contrast, Cosenza (in Calabria – the region that includes Riace) has become a place of almost uninterrupted arrival. This follows long periods of outward migration, both abroad and to north-eastern Italian regions.

In each city, the short-term and long-term housing provision has been a window into governance processes that negotiate, acquiesce and resist what is pursued at national levels. Of course, what is short term and what is long term are not questions that stand apart from the wider migration experience of formal and informal legal status, and the variously conceived ambitions for integration therein. As a key sector of most formulations of integration, housing is, in many respects, the cornerstone of the needs of displaced migrants and refugees. Any discussion of a 'home' as something greater than 'housing' tips into a rich literature which recognises the idea of a home as a lived experience of a self in a locality.[34] Materially, as Phillips put it some years ago, this means that:

> The housing conditions and experiences of refugees clearly play an important role in shaping their sense of security and belonging, and have a bearing on their access to healthcare, education and employment. The ability to access safe, secure and affordable housing is also likely to have an impact on community relations, the level of secondary migration by refugees, and the development of a migrant household's capacity for secure and independent living.[35]

What needs to be equally self-evident is that accommodation is often used as a deterrent rather than as a facilitator of incorporation or integration. The location and quality of accommodation, the triaged nature of its provision or refusal, and the temporary tenure of contracts and forced evictions all speak to this tendency. Evidence of what Wacquant termed 'organisational desertification'[36] – the restriction of networks to prevent social support – is abundant. All of these can be a feature of an asylum-seeking journey, something that often begins with a process designed to hold new arrivals in locations distant to their eventual accommodation. In Cosenza, for example, asylum seekers and refugees are initially housed in 'extraordinary reception centres' (CASs), but then moved into what used to be called the SPRAR network (the Protection System for Asylum and Refuge Seekers), made up of projects that collaborated with the third sector, private sector and local authorities, and which included labour market initiatives. This was a scaled-up version of the Riace model. Building on an existing decentralised reception network involving municipalities and third sector organisations that had been in place since 1999, the Italian SPRAR system came into being in 2002 as a collaboration funded by the Italian Ministry of the Interior with the National Association of Italian Municipalities (ANCI). In the SPRAR model, local authorities that chose to participate in the network applied for short-term (three-year) grants for projects that spanned education, employment and civic life. A policy shift in 2019 by the then Interior Minister has thrown the SPRAR model into uncertainty, and especially its capacity to move beyond the temporary CASs. Asylum seekers no longer move through reception centres to a SPRAR project irrespective of their formal status, but instead remain at the stage of first reception, while only those in receipt of refugee status may leave CASs.

Governing the camp

It is hard not to read such moves as expanding the function of the reception centres as sites of exception,[37] which prevail in the creation of refugee camps, both inside and on the periphery of nation-states' boundaries. A reminder of the power of the nation-state, some of these concerns are taken up in different ways by a number of scholars who address issues almost entirely overlooked by Agamben. This includes the contributions of

Bhambra, Mayblin and El-Enany,[38] among others, who insist that formerly imperial powers' racial hierarchies also had a series of additional functions which come to manifest in the construction, maintenance and afterlife of the camp. All of this is underwritten by inhibiting movement and delegitimising the claims of the residents of former colonies. Together, and as discussed in Chapter Two, these are consistent with patterns of 'making migrants' of those who would otherwise be citizens. As Mayblin observes, it is not a coincidence that restrictions on asylum controls have developed in parallel with demographic shifts among asylum-seeking populations, which, once predominantly White European, since 1990 have increasingly been made up of Black and Brown displaced migrants from the Global South.[39]

Some might ask why this is relevant to the discussion at hand, and one answer is that the resulting regime of racialised and colonial border logics has both national and international effects, and these are no less apparent in cities. Achiume suggests that European border regimes have effectively enacted a form of continental quarantining on states in the Global South,[40] while internally an agenda of what El-Enany has called 'racial (b)ordering'[41] not only seeks to prevent the entry of racialised populations to the state, but also subjects the 'racialised poor' to the 'operation of internal borders' across the local as much as the national. Outwith pandemic conditions, these internal 'everyday bordering'[42] practices to which displaced migrants are subject – coerced immobility, enforced impoverishment, precarious and unsafe accommodation, and spatial 'dumping'[43] – might be understood in the now-familiar terms of public health measures of 'infection control' and social quarantining.

Governing dispossession

The developments described above join an already complex and fractured city-level governance regimes, perhaps illustrated best by how, in Glasgow, asylum seekers are allocated housing on a no-choice basis, in ways that have stymied the capacity of the local state to offer a local approach. Specifically, the accommodation provision available through a dispersal scheme has created competing and complex governance interests that are exacerbated where multi-level governance at the Scottish level comes into conflict with UK-level welfare restrictions and immigration rules. Here, responsibility for both the dispersal scheme (which oversees the accommodation of asylum seekers) and the sponsored refugee scheme (which oversees the resettlement of sponsored refugees) is ultimately held by the UK Government through the Home Office. The schemes rely on two diverging formalised arrangements between UK, devolved and local government for their implementation. The provision of dispersal accommodation, once managed through a direct relationship between the Home Office and participating local authorities (in this case, Glasgow City Council) is also part of a profit-seeking non-state actor partnership.

Such partnerships routinely profit from 'accumulation through dispossession'.[44] The privatisation of these dispersal contracts has not only removed the day-to-day provision and administration of housing for asylum seekers from local authorities, but also policy competences. As such, the type and location of dispersal housing, sizes of asylum-seeking populations within locales, and housing standards no longer come under local urban planning remits. Consequently, Glasgow City Council report very little policy consultation with local authorities, who feel removed from centralised decision-making processes. Meanwhile, gaps in accommodation provision created by the formalised dispersal governance infrastructure, not least asylum seeker destitution, have been almost entirely filled by third sector and grassroots networks. These 'cushion and counteract aspects of … exclusionary national asylum policies … [and] thereby question the legitimacy of national policies and their execution'.[45] It also means that neither the city of Glasgow nor the UK government are the primary providers of accommodation in the city for displaced migrants and refugees – a remarkable state of affairs. The approaches in Glasgow and Calabria are most obviously contrasted with the avowedly top-down approach in Malmö. Here, a 2016 national-level Settlement Law made it mandatory in Sweden for all municipalities to receive refugees, including organising their housing. In this fashion, the numbers of refugees received by the county and municipality was suggested by the Swedish Migration Agency, but the decision on the form of reception was made by each city, in relation to the size of the population, prior experience of refugee reception and labour market opportunities. Malmö, in particular, brings the multi-scalar into view because the city-level approach cannot be understood without appreciating the function of the national-level welfare regime that has embedded a certain kind of solidarity across which local practice moves. Equally, it is important to note that most arrivals settle themselves, without any state or local control, and that a large majority of the municipalities accepted organised settlement long before the Settlement Law. The relatively straightforward landscape in Malmö becomes immensely more complicated in Glasgow and Calabria, but each share in common the continuing and overriding role of the national.

Scaling back and scaling up

In terms of governance processes, at least, the local is thus no less characterised by 'everyday bordering' approaches, something increasingly manifest in the broader preventable harms caused by asylum policies across Europe, and especially so for those people refused the means even to seek refugee status. For, as crises often highlight the problems of existing approaches, so is the case with approaches to asylum and refuge in light of the COVID-19 pandemic. The harrowing circumstances of the creation, conditions in and destruction of the refugee camp in Moira in late 2020 are matched only by the danger of national-level governments breaching the principle of 'non-refoulement' – the cornerstone of international refugee protection[46] – under the shadow of the pandemic. The political rhetoric of some leaders across Europe, meanwhile, has used the pandemic to re-articulate anti-migrant sentiment. The Hungarian Prime Minister Viktor Orbán, for example, told the people of Hungary that 'Our experience is that primarily foreigners brought in the disease, and that it is spreading among foreigners'.[47]

In Italy, former Interior Minister Matteo Salvini claimed that a migrant rescue ship should not have been allowed to dock in Sicily due to the supposed health risk posed by those on board.[48] In a similar vein, the Governor of Sicily, Nello Musumeci, cited fears of migrants spreading COVID-19 when he ordered an emergency decree, subsequently quashed by the Italian government, to close down all hotspots and emergency reception centres. In Greece, the nationalist New Democracy government used COVID-19 as a justification to implement closed camps (which are essentially detention centres) for asylum seekers stranded on various Aegean islands. Elsewhere, in France, Marine Le Pen cited the spread of the coronavirus to justify her renewed push to close France's border with Italy.[49] Alice Weidel, the AfD (Alternative for Germany) leader in the Bundestag, has blamed the spread of the virus on what she called 'the dogma of open borders'.[50] For his part, Santiago Abascal, head of the populist Vox movement in Spain, has been quoted blaming the Socialist government for the spread of COVID-19, because they are, 'so keen to bring down borders [they have] not even taken the minimum measures dictated by common sense'.[51]

If political rhetoric is relevant, then these statements matter in forging norms in public discourse that help to set agendas more broadly and, of course, dovetail with material policy changes. Across the examples discussed here, pandemic conditions have resulted in heightened and tightened curbs on border entry and have arguably facilitated violations of international human rights law. For asylum seekers and refugees already resident in-country, pandemic conditions have also resulted in increased internal restrictions on their mobility and a swift, enforced decline in living conditions within cities. In some cases, politicians have used the pandemic to advance their agenda on displaced migration, taking the opportunity to put in place enhanced border measures to prevent entry into the state. In others, disease prevention controls – social restrictions, quarantining, lockdown – have coincided with existing border controls such as immobilisation, coercive housing and border closures.[52]

At an elementary level, at least 57 countries are making no exception to their travel restrictions for refugees seeking asylum,[53] even though the World Health Organization (WHO) offered clear guidance on the use of quarantines and health screening measures at points of entry for those fleeing persecution. As a result, travel bans and other emergency measures have led to a continual decline in asylum applications in the EU compared to pre-COVID levels, with a registered drop of 43 per cent in March and a subsequent decline of 87 per cent in April 2020 following many countries' suspension of asylum procedures.[54]

This move has left stranded in precarious conditions countless people seeking refuge, and led Filippo Grandi, the UN High Commissioner for Refugees, to argue that 'the core principles of refugee protection are being put to test'.[55] How might things be different in even these most difficult of circumstances? This is specifically a question for cities as they make sense of and come to terms with the 'stop-start' new normal created by the pandemic, and as they attempt to overcome the double challenge of anti-migration hostility as well as the implications of COVID-19. This should not be taken to deny there has been something distinctive under way (seen in the role of the local in general and the city in particular) among responses to the so-called refugee crisis, where civic society, especially, has been a force against racialised social closure. The local is, therefore, a space in which the relationship between civil society and governance becomes a vantage point to observe forms of social (and other) capital at work in migrant and refugee incorporation, including that generated by migrants and refugees *themselves*. In this scenario, and 'whatever the national framework of immigrant incorporation policies', insists Ambrosini,[56] 'the urban level needs to be appreciated as a policy-making field in itself'. This is especially evident in what Miriam Haselbacher has called 'emergency governance'[57] – the immediate arrival response – the longer-term embeddedness of which remains uncertain but relies on the particular character of the city in question.

There is a degree to which what has been described might be understood as part of a longer development in what Brenner has previously characterised as the 'rescaling of statehood'.[58] In this view, there a 'decoupling' between the local and national levels. Scholars such as Myrberg characterise it as 'local governments … shifting from a passive to an active role'.[59] This, however, is to ignore the historical role and status of cities, and to mis-describe the governance dynamics at play. What has been under way is not solely about incommensurability with national-level governance, but about the meshed nature of those dynamics. Yes, cities and local authorities are not merely the sites for national-level processes to filter down, they have a distinctive and historical role to play in the design and implementation of approaches to refuge, but these dynamics are easy to overstate in a type of 'methodological cityism',[60] and especially the argument that the local can address the limitations of the national. Indeed, the local level's room for manoeuvre may be limited and very partial in the area of accommodation provision and support. No less significant, the evacuation of national states from local provision can leave the latter incapable of ensuring elementary provision – including to address homelessness. At its strongest, we might heed Emilsson's insistence that local authorities are, by definition, ultimately 'always subordinate'.[61] This does not appear right either, but Filomeno was surely correct to insist that 'no model of … governance – be it local, national or global – should be reified and explained on its own terms'.[62] The routine racialisation of asylum seekers and refugees should instead direct us to a theorisation of asylum and refuge as part of a wider project of racialisation, something that better helps explain the manufacture and mobilisation of anxieties over the entry and presence of people seeking refuge. This is a sentiment that once more brings both the global and historical into view, and to which we turn next.

SIX

Whiteness and the wreckage of racialisation

A decade has passed since the island of Utøya, not far from the Norwegian capital, in 2011, became the site of the deadliest mass shooting by a single perpetrator, Anders Behring Breivik, in modern history.[1] Breivik's main targets were what he called multiculturalists and cultural Marxists, gunned down for undermining his vision of a White Christian Europe. In many respects, these people were equally the victims of a lethal ideology that has been normalised in mainstream politics, aided and abetted by commentators who draw from a common well. Why have liberal democracies increasingly mainstreamed this White supremacy, and what might have been done to counter it? To answer this question, the chapter brings together a collection of concerns central to this book. Traversing social theory, the history of racialisation, and contemporary politics, it argues that, *after* Utøya, European societies have so far failed to reckon with four social facts. Firstly, it is not the presence of racial minorities that threatens compacts of civil and political peace in Europe but instead a White supremacy that has its provenance in European Christianity, however secularised its appearance. Secondly, White supremacy is not a peripheral activity in European liberal democracies, but often an unstated core. Thirdly, there is a social production of moral indifference manifest in projects of Whiteness that can normalise White supremacy, which is sustained and reproduced in social systems. Fourthly, this is a challenge for White majorities, and just not ethnic and racial minorities, to take ownership of – and to do so for all our sakes.

These may appear provocative statements, but they manifest in plain sight the wreckage of racialisation. The meaning of 'wreckage' in this statement comes from Walter Benjamin. One of many Jewish intellectuals who fled the Nazis, Benjamin tragically committed suicide in 1940 at a port in Catalunya, leaving behind a partial, and – according to some commentators – undiscovered, body of work. Among what was salvaged (by Hannah Arendt no less) was his *Theses on the Philosophy of History*,[2] which his friend Theodore Adorno – who had managed to escape taking the same route earlier – first published on Benjamin's behalf in 1942, with the full abridged English translation coming in Hannah Arendt's version in 1968. Benjamin's work cannot be summarised here, and nor is it limited to his perilous time, but of course what was happening around him was instructive, not least in his discussion of history, of modernity and his understanding of the very idea of European 'progress'. Benjamin famously narrated the tension between history, modernity and progress most poignantly when he referenced the painting by Paul Klee named 'Angelus Novus'. It captivated Benjamin, for in his words it shows an angel looking as though it is about to move away from something on which it is fixed. Its eyes are staring, its mouth is open, its wings are spread. 'This is how one pictures the angel of history', wrote Benjamin,[3] the angel's face is turned toward the past. Where we perceive a chain of events, it sees one single catastrophe which keeps piling wreckage upon wreckage:

> The angel would like to stay, awaken the dead, and make whole what has been smashed. But a storm is blowing ... it is caught in his wings with such violence that the angel can no longer close them. This storm irresistibly propels him into the future to which his back is turned, while the pile of debris before him grows skyward. This storm is what we call progress.[4]

It is difficult to do justice to this passage, but its haunting character is self-evident. It is an allegory, of course, but a powerful one in which something is compelled into a future not of its making, retaining in view the past only as catastrophe at its feet. So, what does this have to do with our discussion? Benjamin's passage has been uppermost in my mind in recent years, perhaps prompted by seeing an installation by the curator Erlend Blakstad Haffner. It is actually a timeline that is mounted on a wall as you approach the former cafe on the island of Utøya, a short ferry crossing from Oslo. Counting not years, not months nor even weeks, this timeline details in minutes and seconds the final anxious text messages between children on the island and their parents on the Norwegian mainland. The children, of course, were among the victims of Breivik's terror at a summer camp held by the youth wing of the Norwegian Labour Party. 'As we all know', he wrote in his manifesto shared online before the attacks, 'the root of Europe's problems is the lack of cultural self-confidence and nationalism.'[5]

The timeline rests among a number of buildings preserved to commemorate the victims by turning the space into a teaching and learning centre to support antiracism work in Norway and beyond. In all, 69 young people were killed on the island, and a further 8 people perished in the associated bomb attacks in Oslo. Many others were very seriously injured. The learning centre incorporates the cafe – a building where 13 people were killed, and where 19 people found refuge. The outer layer is made up of 495 wooden slats, one for every person on the island that survived the attack, and the glazed inside layer is framed by 69 columns that pay tribute to every fatality. Having worked with antiracism activists there, taking the same ferry as Breivik to cross the short stretch of water, and treading the same ground in the climb up to the cafe, I can only testify to the impression it leaves, and how Benjamin's words[6] reverberate, not least the desire 'to stay, awaken the dead, and make whole what has been smashed'.

If we focus on the nature of the storm and the wreckage it heralds in our moment in history, we see that the success of the commemoration at Utøya is matched only by our broader failure to heed its warning. This involves a social production of moral indifference which tacitly accepts the privileges that come to the beneficiaries of this Whiteness – as a social, political and historical project. As such, we return full circle to the discussion set out in Chapter One, to deepen our understanding of Whiteness as a 'project' – something that is constructed – and from which many people who may define themselves as White today have been excluded in the near past. Whiteness and people who self-define as 'White', therefore, are not the same thing; this chapter is about the social, political and historical dynamics of a racial project. The burden of facing up to Whiteness as a 'project', however, has to be taken up more by White people than is presently the case. Recognising this is key to sifting through the wreckage of White supremacy. The first part of the argument is straightforward.

Wreckage upon wreckage ...

Over a number of years, it has not been uncommon for me to receive invitations, with the very best of intentions, to discuss – and perhaps defend – the concept of Islamophobia, and to theoretically or empirically weigh up the merits and de-merits of this category, for others to arbitrate – perhaps adjudicate – on its relative utility. Having spilt a great deal of ink on this topic,[7] I find it appropriate to refuse such invitations and instead to point colleagues to several decades of compelling scholarship from people whose work spans disciplines and methodologies in their telling of Islamophobia. I do this because the overlooked challenge is, instead, to try to lift our gaze from the racialised in order also see the racialiser. The need for this analytical pivot, this reversal of the telescope, could not be more crucial.

In recent years, commentators have become more alert to the fact that White supremacy kills White people too, as illustrated in Germany's justice minister Christine Lambrecht concluding that 'Far-Right terror is the biggest threat to our democracy right now',[8] in a statement that followed Tobias Rathjen's killing of nine people in Hanau, near the city of Frankfurt. The events that took place on the island of Utøya, and what has happened subsequently in places including Christchurch (New Zealand), San Diego, Hanau and elsewhere since Utøya, are intimately related. Indeed, the University of Maryland's Global Terrorism Database (GTD) recorded a 320 per cent increase in far-right terrorism between 2013 and 2018,[9] and helps us to chart how Utøya has featured in the shootings of White supremacists spanning the Wisconsin Gurdwara shooting, the murder of UK MP Jo Cox in 2016 by a member of the far right, to Christchurch and beyond. Of course, in referring to recent and past events, we must wish to avoid a kind of 'politicking'. As Hage has argued, we must speak with the memory of victims and survivors in mind.[10] They include Mucaad Ibrahim. At three years old, he was the youngest victim of the Christchurch mosque shootings. Smart beyond his tender years, his family described him as, 'A Muslim Kiwi who was full of energy, love and happiness'.[11] Or from San Diego, Lori Kaye, aged 60, who died after throwing herself in front of the rabbi when the gunman opened fire at the Jewish community centre.[12] Or Simon Saebo, 18, a student from Troms county who was among those who perished on Utøya.[13]

In many respects these people were the victims of a lethal ideology as much as they were victims of any individual. These were not the actions of lone wolves. Brenton Tarrant, the Australian who gunned down 51 adults and children during Friday prayers at two mosques in Christchurch,[14] chalked Breivik's name on his weapons and live-streamed his attack to many of Breivik's Facebook followers.[15] Tarrant also made prominent on his weapons the insignia '14 WORDS' – referencing the motto propagated by David Lane (an influential White supremacist who died in a US prison in 2007) 'We must secure the existence of our people and a future for white children'.[16] Adopted by supporters of the 45th President of the United States, in Charlottesville, Virginia, the 14 words were rendered down to five: the slogan 'You will not replace us'.[17]

The underlying belief for Breivik, Tarrant and others is that non-Whites and non-Christians (especially Muslims) are invaders, intent on replacing the White majority in Europe and the West more broadly through a numerical challenge, political subversion and cultural domination. One year after Utøya, the French writer Renaud Camus published his bestselling text *Le Grand Remplacement* [*The Great Replacement*],[18] which has become a guiding tenet for many. Its thesis that Europeans are on the verge of 'replacement' by 'non-Europeans' has found immense traction in many countries, and it is the very flagstone of the transnational organisation Generation Identity which is very active on UK university campuses.

What is, of course, alarming is that since Utøya this conspiracy theory has become central to the public discourse of political parties who are now part of the mainstream in European politics, including some who hold office in national, regional and local government. This includes the Freedom Party of Austria, the French National Front (renamed National Rally), the Swedish Democrats, Fidesz in Hungary, Finns Party, the Danish People's Party, Italy's Lega Nord, the New Flemish Alliance in Belgium, and the AfD in Germany, among others. As Mondon and Winter document in *Reactionary Democracy*,[19] such electoral success offers case studies in how White supremacy has been normalised in mainstream politics, aided and abetted by commentators and, indeed, analysts who revel in promoting the populism they claim to study.

Racial injustice as moral indifference

Despite these entanglements, however, these political mobilisations of Whiteness can be seen and named – they have a performative character which the late historian Tony Judt described as 'one long scream of resentment'.[20] What this doesn't explain is how they have been incrementally centred and found a broader resonance. This is where we encounter the harder explanatory challenge. For we cannot properly answer this question unless we are willing to grapple with the banal repositories that enable it. In so doing we need to hold in our minds two projects of Whiteness for, in addition to supremacy, Whiteness also operates implicitly through the kinds consensus that prevail in White majority societies; what Dyre once termed as 'seeming not to be anything in particular',[21] and what Mills described as a 'cognitive phenomena' that allows White majorities to 'disappear as a "race" and simply become coextensive with the human. Or alternatively phrased, whiteness becomes humanness. Issues of "race" are then tacitly or overtly thought of by whites as really having to do with nonwhites as a group, not the "raceless" and "universal" whites.'[22]

Du Bois once termed this a 'public and psychological wage'[23] and, later still, McIntosh would come to call it a 'knapsack' that is carried with you.[24] Harder to name than explicitly 'White nationalist' movements, it is this social production of moral indifference that underwrites so much else. What is being described relies on disinterest in knowing how 'a system of illicit racial empowerment and disablement inherited from the past may still be at work, reproducing unfair privilege and handicap at different racial poles through a wide variety of interlocking societal mechanisms'.[25]

Some commentators say they are so weary from trying make visible what is obvious, that they have ceased trying, perhaps most succinctly put in the title of Reni Eddo-Lodge's *Why I'm No Longer Talking to White People About Race*.[26] The last point is important, for while struggle for racial justice is in large measure a case of 'the oppressed [having] to teach the oppressors their mistakes',[27] any account of this topic must not ignore minoritised refusal.

For what is being described here is a constant negotiation against a kind of capital, what Troy Duster elaborates as being 'deeply embedded in the routine structures of economic and political life. From ordinary service at restaurants, to far greater access to bank loans to simple *police-event-free* driving – all these things have come unreflectively with the territory of being white'.[28] To put it another way, and to quote Du Bois once more, 'we do not really associate with each other, without also associating with our ideas of each other'.[29] Whiteness here is a structured norm against which others are valued. This is not straightforward, but it is an error in formalistic inquiry to deny it in a way that negates the linkages.

One example is the suggestion that we can only describe systems of racism, but cannot attribute any agency to individuals that benefit from and preserve such systems. Opposition to these terms might be viewed as an illustration of how 'political strategies are encoded within … academic debates'.[30] Perhaps this is inevitable insofar as value-free inquiry is implausible and, in posing 'strong questions', undesirable. That should not imply that searching criticisms made in good faith seek to deny issues of racism. Instead, one explanation for the discomfort sensed in some social science responses to the discussion of White supremacy and privilege, respectively, probably takes us to what Barnor Hesse famously described as 'racism's conceptual double bind'.[31] By this he meant that for a number of scholars their association of racism 'with some form of extremism or exceptionalism' prevents them from seeing 'something more conventional and mainstream'.[32] Race scholars, of course, view things differently. Yet, on the whole, mainstream social science has been late in accepting this. As Twine and Gallagher put it:

> Throughout much of the twentieth-century mainstream, white social scientists did not focus on the institutions that created, reproduced and normalized white supremacy. The focus that guided the academy primarily concerned itself with the pathology of racist individuals rather than the structural forces that produced racist social systems.[33]

But if social scientists have been at fault, then so have historians. For who gets to benefit from this category has been far from straightforward, because the project of Whiteness has not been consistent. For example, there are many groups who today would self-define and be defined by others as White, but who have not been so in the past. As we learned from Ignatiev[34] in Chapter One, we might think of the Irish in America and indeed in Britain, or indeed of Italians and other immigrants to America, who became 'White' over time, something which illustrates the ways Whiteness has changed as a project. There are a variety of literatures that chart this, but equally we should be in no doubt the provenance of these racial categories was always firmly weighted in favour of Europeans in the end, for 'The white colour holds the first place', the 19th-century physiologist and anthropologist Johann Blumenbach wrote. 'I have taken the name of this variety from Mount Caucasus, both because its neighbourhood, and especially its southern slope, produces the most beautiful race of men.' The 'Caucasian variety', by which he meant Europeans, were 'colour white, cheeks rosy; hair brown or chestnut-coloured; head subglobular; face oval, straight, its parts moderately defined, forehead smooth, nose narrow, slightly hooked, mouth small'.[35]

Like many of his contemporaries, he was also, of course, setting up a hierarchy. While appearing comical to us today, these were taxonomies that established hierarchies that White Europeans would use to service (in simple and complex ways) what Marimba Ani called 'the Maafa' – the horror of the transatlantic slave trade: perhaps 12 million Africans trafficked, with two million men, women, and children killed in the capture, on the voyage, or soon after, and the survivors sold into bondage.[36] Theirs is a story, as Hartman described, that is not matched by a corresponding archive equivalent to the event, and so remains a 'story predicated upon impossibility – listening for the unsaid, translating misconstrued words, and refashioning disfigured lives – and intent on achieving an impossible goal: redressing the violence that produced numbers, ciphers, and fragments of discourse, which is as close as we come to a biography of the captive and the enslaved'.[37]

That such indescribable horror is unaccompanied by normative public commemoration resembling that afforded to national remembrance, for example, is connected to what is deemed worthy of our formal archives, and precisely the reason that Lorde asked us to 'remember the ghosts of those that came before us, that we carry within ourselves'.[38] Numbers cannot do justice to either their stories or those of the more than 60 million who starved to death under British rule during the Indian famines, and where at least one British Viceroy – Lord Lytton – actively promoted the winnowing of Indian populations.[39] These horrors are, of course, integral to the present-day accumulated wealth of a number of European societies, and against which the upset of renaming buildings or taking down statues might be set. Importantly, even these racial hierarchies relied upon a prior European repertory of knowledge – something which takes us to the very first recorded ideas of race.

Present beginnings

This chapter cannot do justice to the understanding of where racial categories come from, but we should recognise that there is a lively and ongoing dispute among colleagues on this matter. Some chart our ideas of race to particular events, such as the arrival of Europeans in the Americas, or the Atlantic slave trade, or later still in the creation of a colonial–modern infrastructure of imperialism. What is of most relevance to us in these accounts is the emphasis they attribute to European Christianity in the formation of race, and which requires a kind of genealogical inquiry that is otherwise forgotten because of how secularism comes to foreclose or obscure the ways in which Christianity is foundational to European race-making: both historically and presently. This is the argument recently made by Jansen and Meer,[40] which takes a different course to reach the same destination plotted in this Jennings' thesis *The Christian Imagination: Theology and the Origins of Race*.[41] In this, Jennings centres the well-known account of the abduction and arrival in Portugal in 1444 of over two hundred West Africans, and 'the beginning moments of the trans-Atlantic slave trade', and the 'auctioning of bodies without regard to any form of human connection'. What is key for Jennings is that this act is carried out 'inside the communitas fidelium [community of the faithful]' where 'an unchanging God wills to create Christians out of slaves and slaves out of black bodies that will someday, the Portuguese hope, claim to be Christians'.[42]

Other narrations of what has been termed the 'race-religion nexus',[43] and the racialisation of religion,[44] make a different link with Christianity to argue that the provenance of race can also be understood through the racialisation of religion in early modern Europe. For example, in Sebastián de Covarrubias's infamous 16th-century dictionary, race was in fact conjoined with the words 'blood' and 'religion'.[45] Indeed, there is ample evidence that religious culture and physical traits were deemed as co-constitutive of a racial category that flowed into Atlantic slavery and early colonial encounters, even prior to the Reconquista when in 1492 the Catholics monarchs took over Muslim Spain.[46] In fact, it was at this point in Spain that the idea of 'blood purity' was first invented as a means to argue that those Jews and Muslims who had converted to Christianity were still racially different because their religion was corporeal – it was in their blood. All this is to take issue with a central part of the highly influential 'racial formation' thesis put forward by

Omi and Winant. In focusing on the place of race in culture, economics and law, these authors maintain that a 'conception of race does not occur until the rise of Europe and the arrival of Europeans in the Americas'.[47] Theirs is a wide-ranging account, and it is most relevant to our discussion because of how they limit hostility toward Muslims and Jews as expressions of religious bigotry, in the following manner:

> [T]he hostility and suspicion with which Christian Europe viewed its two significant non-Christian 'others' – the Muslims and Jews – cannot be viewed as more than a rehearsal for racial formation, since these antagonisms, for all their bloodletting and chauvinism, were always and everywhere religiously interpreted.[48]

These authors are not alone, and are joined, for example, by Quijano, for whom the idea of race 'does not have a known history before the colonization of America', since 'the racial axis has a colonial origin and character'.[49] For others, including Mignolo: 'Racism, as we sense it today, was the result of ... conceptual inventions of imperial knowledge.'[50] Each share in common not only that coloniality is the crucible of race, but also that the race concept is most substantively forged in modernity, or in Gilroy's terms: 'modernity transformed the ways "race" was understood and acted upon'.[51] There are a number of literatures with which we might develop this point. Gilroy is an important example, and there are several places in his repertoire where this might be taken up. Perhaps strangely, his majestic *Black Atlantic: Modernity and Double Consciousness* does not make this an explicit focus, concentrating specifically on the ways in which 'the social and political subordination of blacks and other non-European peoples does not generally feature in debates about ... modernity'.[52] That book, then, is one very compelling corrective to the structured oversight. It is instead elsewhere, in *Between Camps*, where Gilroy's fullest elaboration of the points raised above arguably come through. This includes his reading that: 'Although it is not acknowledged as often as it should be, the close connection between "race" and modernity can be viewed with a special clarity if we allow our understanding of modernity to travel, to move with the workings of the great imperial systems.'[53]

So, there is what we can call an elective affinity between empire, race and modernity. My response to this is not to deny that modernity has a particular formulation of race, but simply to suggest this is a formulation that is underwritten and made possible by pre-modern Christian characteristics that are pulled through, and that without these the modernist conception of racialisation or race-making cannot hold. For example, when Islam is first encountered in Europe, 'the Prophet Mohammed (with his Jewish parents and heretical teacher)' is embodied as a dark-skinned, Satanic menace.[54] Note that Pope Urban II's exhortation at Clermont in 1095, to take up the cross in the First Crusade, included his description of how the Holy Land and much of Byzantium had been taken by 'the Turks', an 'accursed race', a 'slave of the demons', as he urged his co-religionists 'to exterminate this vile race from the lands of our brethren'.[55]

Modernity in this sense offers 'one of many reorganisations and rearticulations of the meaning of race that have occurred throughout the centuries'.[56] All that needs to be shown here is that race bears pre-modern antecedents in Christianity. There are multiple examples to sustain this view, and both Hund and Isaac dwell on this at some length (although they disagree on the geographical provenance of race).[57] If one shares the view that modernist formulations of race are at least in part assembled from pre-modern components then, following Mills, 'the neatness of the present periodization will have to be given up' and, as 'a corollary, the case for making race a subject of inquiry across various disciplines would be greatly strengthened and made more urgent'.[58]

What is being argued is that while the racial formation thesis might capture many of the mechanics of racialisation, the account needs to commence earlier to recognise how racialised categories have saturated cultural portrayals of Muslims and Jews, endowing each with characteristics that offered 'reassurance that their difference could be easily identified as non-Christians'.[59] The point is about antecedents rather than perfect symmetry, and in different ways both Nabil Matar and James Shapiro have provided a rich discussion of how ideas of the Moor and the Jew featured in Elizabethan England,[60] and in the period's most celebrated author we find illustrative depictions of each, namely, Shakespeare's characterisation of the tragically violent Othello and the shrewd and sinister Shylock.

While each are replete with redeeming qualities, and even by today's standards imbued with striking degrees of ambiguity, they nonetheless make sense as racialised affectations of their time. In the case of the former, the moral panic over Moors in London is well documented. Popular depictions in which Muslims 'raged and lusted, killed their children or enslaved and brutalized Christians'[61] were widely circulated. In the case of Jewish minorities in Elizabethan England, who were yet to be formally readmitted following their expulsion in 1290, the character of Shylock was at least partly sustained by a mythology of the 'threat of Jews circumcising Englishmen, taking Christian servants, and racially contaminating the nation'.[62] The important point is that, for Shakespeare no less than his audiences, these ideas of the Moor and the Jew were shorthand for non-Christian racial difference. In this respect it was Christianity which provided the constituting repertoires of difference for the Western world, meaning that the category of race was co-constructed with religion: a genealogy which implicates the formation of the race concept in the overlapping racialisation of religious subjects today. Thus, the later arrival of 19th-century racial taxonomies drew on a deep well of European Christian thought – the methods were different but the hierarchies the same, and heavily reliant on an underlying Christian teleology. The challenge in reading these accounts is once more to connect racial logics to racial projects, namely, and returning to Goldberg, to trace what he calls the 'inter-coursing connectivities of the racial',[63] by which is meant that instead of just comparing and contrasting, we need to connect more than we have been doing. In this instance, in this book, the challenge is to connect the uses of Whiteness to one another.

Why do these genealogies matter? If the answer is not already apparent, we are talking here about lethal racial projects, which in Europe have had to be actively made and remade – and that is what we are in the midst of today, just as we have been before. This is illustrated in writers who anxiously debated the 'decline' of a White Europe in the late 19th and early 20th centuries. People, like Benjamin Kidd in his *Social Evolution* and *Principles of Western Civilisation*,[64] wrote endlessly about White European decline. Kidd was writing at a time when the British Empire reigned over nearly a quarter of planet's landmass, and other European powers exploited the people and territories they had taken. His anxiety is wrapped up in how Whiteness served as a form of rationality that fashioned the world in its own image. Empire and colonialism are thus understood as natural states of international relations and indicative of human progress.

It is remarkable to find so much here that is contemporary: especially the demography panic, which constantly returns, and is promoted vigorously by people taken seriously in the mainstream of public discourse.[65] A *contemporary* pioneer account comes not from Camus[66] but in the bestselling polemic from Mark Steyn *America Alone*,[67] which was especially successful at popularising the 'Eurabia Myth':

> Arriving at a time of demographic, political, and cultural weakness, Muslims are profoundly changing Europe. Islam has youth and will, Europe has age and welfare. Put differently, pre-modern Islam beats post-modern Christianity. Much of the Western world will not survive the twenty-first century, and much of it will effectively disappear within our lifetimes, including many if not most European countries ...[68]

Steyn moves on to offer the following analysis, and makes the blood-curdling prescription:

> Why did Bosnia collapse into the worst slaughter in Europe since World War Two? In the thirty years before the meltdown, Bosnian Serbs had declined from 43 percent to 31 percent of the population, while Bosnian Muslims had increased from 26 percent to 44 percent. In a democratic age, you can't buck demography – except through civil war. The Serbs

figured that out – as other Continentals will in the years ahead: if you can't outbreed the enemy, cull 'em. The problem that Europe faces is that Bosnia's demographic profile is now the model for the entire continent.[69]

Not so outrageous as to prevent the novelist Martin Amis repeating this trope, soon after being appointed professor of creative writing at Manchester:

They're also gaining on us demographically at a huge rate. A quarter of humanity now and by 2025 they'll be a third. Italy's down to 1.1 child per woman. We're just going to be outnumbered ... There's a definite urge – don't you have it? – to say, 'The Muslim community will have to suffer until it gets its house in order.[70]

How Muslims respond to this varies, for Muslim identities are not the sum of these framings, and resist being purely understood through them, principally by asserting modes of self-identification.[71] In this respect, we could say Muslims have understood that 'their personal troubles cannot be solved merely as "private troubles"', as C. Wright Mills so memorably puts it, 'but must be understood in terms of public issues – and in terms of the problems of history making'.[72] Yet while Muslims today are not the passive objects of racialisation, they are the objects of it nonetheless, and the racialisation problematic advanced in this book allows us to understand the ways in which there is an attribution of 'meaning to somatic characteristics', in a way that 'presumes a kind of anthropological theory' about Muslim difference in Europe.[73] This is something that spans both cognitive and systemic tendencies, as well as their interactions with each other, for example what we call institutional racism. These are not historical concerns, even though this chapter has encouraged a historical understanding, as illustrated by Kaufmann and his agenda-setting *Whiteshift: Populism, Immigration and the Future of White Majorities*,[74] which advances a racial project that shares mechanisms with earlier projects where groups who are marked as Other routinely find themselves on the other side of the boundary of 'us'. This includes the author's advocacy of a cultural points system on immigration that would rank migrants on their similarity to existing groups; an argument in favour of long-term refugee camps instead of entry into Europe; second-tier citizenship for undocumented migrants, many of whom may have been born, educated and worked in their society, specifically in order to deny them membership in the nation and the right to vote.

The argument of this chapter, and indeed the book, is that we must understand there is not a normal, reasonable amount of White supremacy that can be accommodated, to allay fears of Muslims, refugees, Blacks or any racialised minority. Lethal ideas should not be deemed normal or reasonable to help to give majority-White populations an explanation for inequality, or hardship, or simply the changing nature of their societies. Those who make a virtue of these arguments traffic in ideas of racial hierarchy to blame systemic failures on racial minorities. They illustrate why naming and thinking critically about Whiteness as an object of extremism is only half the challenge, and one that, after Utøya, we have so far failed to reckon with. Our moment requires that we *must* talk about Whiteness as an everyday project of privilege, and not just about White supremacy as a fringe element. This is not simple; it necessitates White majority discomfort and it is harder to name than explicitly 'White nationalist' movements – but it is in this we can find social production of moral indifference that underwrites so much else. To ignore it is to be propelled – much like Benjamin's Angel of History – once more into a future not of our making.

SEVEN

Rethinking the future: affect, orders and systems

The future of racial justice has a very long past, something that is patterned by failure and success, in ways that confound the optimism of inevitable racial justice in time. In this concluding chapter we consider how we might learn from all that has preceded, so that we may forge a route to a different future if there is a collective will to do so. Perhaps this requires imagining a different *present* as well as future, and here there is a rich and engaging tradition within one branch of history that explores what are called 'subjunctive conditionals', the alternative histories that might have occurred had other things been different.[1] This book has not pursued this tradition for it has, instead, taken seriously the notion that we can learn from system-wide patterns. In one respect, this view confirms what Berlant described as a 'compulsion to repeat optimism', something which heralds the 'possibility that [it] also risks having to survive, once again, disappointment'.[2] This makes it different from a utopian approach or something akin to Levitas's outline of what she calls 'an imaginary reconstitution of society'.[3] Nor is it a purely descriptive exercise detailing what has happened where, and to whom. On the contrary, what the book has very much tried to do is encourage us to grasp that while the specific events of our time may be distinctive, they necessarily reflect 'a past which in some sense is still living in the present'.[4] This framing is necessary because the pursuit of racial justice in our present moment cannot be understood in and of itself, and this book departs therefore from Mills' insistence that 'a *philosophical* investigation into race need not take a stand on many of these causal questions'.[5] The argument here is that the pursuit of racial justice is not only a moral question but a profoundly affective social and political struggle, one that is multi-temporal in simultaneously reflecting struggle over time, which must not be overlooked in any narration of racial *injustice*.

Adopting this approach allows us to grasp the 'cruel optimism'[6] inherent in the pursuit of racial justice, and in which *possibilities* become *impossibilities*. It makes apparent the mutual dependence of affective experiences of racial projects that sustain systemic racial injustices, including the possibilities for transformation that racial injustice creates, the 'second sight' realised in everyday scenarios where responding to racial injustice probes deeper meanings and contradictions of a racialised experience.[7] It is found in the words of the Doreen and Neville Lawrence which continue to echo down through the years and join the chorus of ongoing 'racial battle fatigue' nearly 30 years after their son Stephen's murder in 1993.[8] The argument that has been advanced across the previous chapters of this book rests on a critique of the belief in the inevitable progress in racial justice, that things are getting or will get better in time. What has been charted across a number of sectors points to the contrary: that we see regression as well as advance. What Berlant's motif helps us to narrate is that, however shocking racial equalities may appear when observed at one moment, in our pursuit of racial justice we have, as a society, adapted to 'a notion of systemic crisis or "crisis ordinariness"'.[9] Here, and as the COVID-19 disparities discussed in Chapter Four highlight, '[t]he extraordinary always turns out to be an amplification of something in the work ...'.[10]

What the preceding chapters have been insisting, moreover, and a key argument animating this book, is that we need to take a more systemic approach when we discuss otherwise seemingly disparate concerns in ancillary social spheres – whether these manifest in organisations, sectors, institutions or elsewhere – by specifically broadening the aperture to take in the nature of the whole. Once we do so we can appreciate the regularity of racial injustice, and how it can flourish without the need for choreographed and pre-meditated racist intentionality. At work in these outcomes are the mechanics of racialisation that operate across different racial projects. Connecting with Feagin's ideas about the 'white racial frame'[11] allows us to grasp how systems are 'embodied', and not apart from racial projects. The argument advanced here is that systems, identities and societies bear the imprints of older racial injustices that are not merely restated but re-articulated in ways that may be novel, and yet share common properties with how other racial projects have been curated and sustained.

How racial justice may advance in light of these conditions routinely shows that 'surface-level changes are widely cited and often become a distraction from more ingrained structural oppressions and deepening inequalities that continue'.[12] From political rhetoric to public policy and indeed law, the cruel optimism of racial justice perseveres through the systemic and fatal inequalities elaborated a length in earlier chapters. This, in the end, may best explain Martin Luther King's reflection: 'I must confess that that dream that I had that day has in many points turned into a nightmare.'[13] Seeing racial injustice as conventional and not exceptional, therefore, and as capable of being mapped across social systems by paying attention to racial projects, we would be better placed to grasp the nature of the challenge we face. As Chapters Three and Four detail, the inequalities that flow from these injustices have a long tail, and so show another way in which we need to get beyond novelty – the issues are not new, simply because they reoccur, as the discussion of racial disparities and COVID-19 illustrate. Indeed, the effects of racism on what are presented as health outcomes remain insufficiently recognised precisely because there is an unwillingness to grasp a longer account of how experiences of racial discrimination are linked to numerous physical and mental health outcomes. These outcomes cannot be explained in isolation, for they co-occur and sequentially lead to and reflect deepening inequalities in many domains. As Liebman and colleagues put it: 'the spectacular cruelty that the COVID-19 pandemic illuminates is not new, highlighting bio- and necropolitical capitalist landscapes long in the making. Yet the virus exposes how these dynamics are constantly in flux as capital struggles to reproduce itself and makes unstable alliances with the State.'[14]

As stated at the outset, however, this should not encourage a totalising approach that forecloses agency, minimises resistance and refusal, or collapses racial minorities into mere objects of racist social systems. For, as Milsum put it more than half a century ago, while 'systems have some stability which resists the initiation of change', this can only be maintained 'until some threshold of forcing stress is reached, after which growth seems to occur explosively'.[15] Perhaps our present moment of accumulated struggle promises just such a shift: the breach of a threshold, something we will only materialise as more than a promise when we cease to pretend racial injustice is an aberration in an otherwise race-less, meritocratic society; when the emphasis is on the barrel and not a few bad apples; and when White people, too, are willing take ownership of racial inequalities and understand these as an integral part of society. Doing so requires White majorities to relinquish an assumed innocence that refuses 'not only to acknowledge the other but to acknowledge that we enact this denial; it is disowning (our connection to) social facts we in some sense know, such as the exercise of power, the practice of inequality, or their benefits'.[16] This will have to take in the multi-scalar and not retreat to local and national imaginations alone, and be able to speak to the ways 'human bodies are turned into a commodity to be bought, trafficked or stored by multi-scalar agencies, including detention centres [that are] part of a process of accumulation through dispossession'.[17] A key impediment to this is the social production of moral indifference which tacitly accepts the privileges that come to the beneficiaries of Whiteness – as a social, political and historical project which 'unwittingly' sanctions the 'production and exploitation of group-differentiated vulnerability to premature death'.[18] Whiteness and people who self-define as 'White' therefore are not the same thing, but the burden of facing up to Whiteness as a 'project' must be taken up more by White people than is presently the case, and they must do so for all our sakes. As earlier chapters show, what is important here is the long shadow of how past constructs of Whiteness that were 'society-led', would, in practice, rationalise 'to whom the state and its associated community considered itself to be responsible'.[19] This is something which remains overlooked in the study of nations and nationalism, in particular, and not least in how "'the nation" often stands as the mirror to which imperial identities are reflected back'.[20] For an academic, it makes sense that we should continue to believe that the 'weight of historical scholarship and empirical inquiry [must] eventually make itself felt, and with the support of a broader political movement, one might reasonably hope that this would eventually have an influence on the minds, and maybe even the hearts'.[21] Of course, this is the very cruelty in our optimism named as such throughout. Perhaps in the final analysis this is a utopian vision after all, but as Mercuse once suggested, 'when truth cannot be realised within the established order, it always appears to the latter as mere utopia'.[22]

It is imperative to reiterate that the concern with social systems, and how they scale up racial projects in ways that draw on recurrent racial mechanisms, must not be taken as evidence of futility or impossibility in the desire to hope for a better future. If this is the same motive that binds us into a cruel optimism presently, this need not be our future too. Certainly, we must look to the past, not least 'to battle the pernicious ideological scaffolding of white supremacy effectively',[23] but much like Benjamin's messianic angel of history,[24] this is at the same time a future-oriented concern. The social agency implied in these ways of understanding the problem of racial injustice is also present in other literatures that might be characterised as flanking the discussion of cruel optimism. One concerns the possibility of 'tragedy' and includes Cornel West's majestic discussion of how tragedy can be a vehicle for collective action. For West, this has been borne out in the 'tragic action with revolutionary intent, usually reformist consequences, and always visionary outlook' that he observes in African American political history.[25] In certain respects, his argument inverts Steiner's consciously religious statement that tragedy arises 'out of the sense that necessity is blind',[26] and so further illustrates the dynamics of White Christianity discussed in Chapter Six. Unlike Berlant's account, it is harder to uncouple West's discussion from its provenance, specifically the forms of Christianity, Marxism and American pragmatism that he draws together in his narration of African American struggle. West also, however, shares something with the second flank of concerns in the discussion of hope.[27] This, too, has a theological feature, specifically in the function of hope as it was elaborated by 13th-century Catholic theologian Thomas Aquinas. In this tradition, faith and hope are not synonymous, for '[w]hereas faith teaches the general possibility of eternal salvation, hope personally appropriates that shared belief as something that is possible'.[28] Naturally, this articulation of hope as a theological virtue is divine, and struggles to function outside of these obvious parameters. Still, something of this appeal is signalled in Back's distinction between 'a worldly hope and cruel or unconditional optimism', and the kinds of reorientation to 'attentiveness' this invites, working outwards from the world as we find it.[29] Reflecting, in particular, on the sentiment – often attributed to Gramsci – on the pessimism of the mind contra an optimism of the will, his injunction is that: 'Hopeful possibility and action can be sustained without necessarily being hostage to the belief that everything is going to improve or turn out well ... This seemingly paradoxical entanglement is a way of holding to the world that combines critical reflection and attentiveness.'[30]

The latter must include a reckoning of the social and, of course, moral cost of racial injustice, but also support the necessary imagination that takes us through and beyond understandable despair. The burden of this labour is presently asymmetrical, landing disproportionately on racialised minorities who can see as self-evident these truths as they manifest across social systems. A fundamental rebalancing of this is only possible when the beneficiaries of the social production of moral indifference recognise that this is their load to bear as well. Perhaps this is the necessary first part in recognising what Lorde described as 'old blueprints of expectation and response, old structures of oppression', and which 'must be altered at the same time as we alter the living conditions which are a result of those structures'.[31] For only then might the cruel optimism of racial justice transform into a justified perseverance of hope.

Notes

Chapter One

1. Cohn and Quealy (2020); Holt and Sweitzer (2020); Bailey and Sigona (2020).
2. Collingwood (2013, p 97).
3. Fanon (1968, p 23).
4. Mills (2018, p 69).
5. Mills (1997); (2007).
6. Rawls (1999 [1971]).
7. Mills (2013, p 2).
8. Ibid (original emphasis).
9. Berlant (2011)
10. Berlant (2011, p 227).
11. Hartman (2007).
12. Douglass et al (2018, p 1).
13. Writing knowingly about the possibilities of racial justice as an ideal, Mills (2013, p 20) argues that racial injustice 'breaches the norm of equal personhood and respect upon which liberalism qua liberalism is supposed to rest.... Racial injustice is, most fundamentally, a refusal to respect equal personhood, whether in the original rights violations or in the legacy of such violations. Racial injustice is antiliberal.'
14. Baldwin (1962).
15. Berlant (2011, p 2).
16. Berlant (2011, pp 121–2).
17. Lorey (2012, p 45), quoted in Bargetz (2015).
18. Bargetz (2015, p 590).
19. Ibid.
20. Ahmed (2004, p 119).
21. Meer (2018a).
22. Du Bois (1999 [1903], pp 10–11).
23. Du Bois (1971, p 416).
24. Seamster and Ray (2018, p 316).
25. Berlant (2011, p 263).
26. Logan (2020, p ix).
27. For example, being Commissioner on the Royal Society of Edinburgh (RSE) Post-COVID-19 Futures Inquiry (2020–21); an adviser to the Scottish Government's COVID-19 and Ethnicity Expert Reference Group (2020); a member of the Scottish Government COVID-19 Public

Engagement Expert Advisory Group (2020–21); a Race Equality Advisor (Scotland) to the UK Cabinet Office's Race Disparity Audit (2018; see https://www.gov.uk/government/publications/race-disparity-audit); an academic adviser in the drafting of Scotland's Race Equality Framework (2016); a member of the Evidence Group of the New Scots Integration Strategy, a part of British Council's Outreach Program (2012), and a collaborator on the United Nations Global Compact on Migration (2017).

[28] Back (2020).

[29] Hage (2020).

[30] Quoted in Macpherson (1999, para 4:12).

[31] Butler (2004, p 22).

[32] Lawrence (2020, p 4).

[33] Ibid.

[34] House of Commons and House of Lords Joint Committee on Human Rights (2020).

[35] Written evidence from Just for Kids Law/Children's Rights Alliance (RHR0022) to the Joint Committee on Human Rights Inquiry on Black People, Racism and Human Rights: see https://committees.parliament.uk/writtenevidence/12266/html

[36] Youth Justice Statistics (2018/19, p 42).

[37] UK Government (2021, para 24).

[38] Berlant (2011, p 1).

[39] Including: the 'Windrush Lessons Learned' review – see Gentleman (2020); the 2017 race disparity audit (spanning nearly all public sectors) – see Muir et al (2017); the 2017 Lammy report (looking specifically at criminal justice) – see Bowcott and Dodd (2017); the 2017 McGregor-Smith review (focusing on labour markets) – see Allen (2017); and the 2017 Angiolini review (investigating deaths in police custody) – see Dodd (2017).

[40] Olsen et al (2020, p 14).

[41] Home Office (2021).

[42] CRED (2021, p 8).

[43] CRED (2021, p 11).

[44] Berlant (2011, p 10).

[45] Ibid.

[46] Berlant (2011, p 1).

[47] Macpherson (1999), para 2.17).

[48] Bonilla-Silva (1997, p 474).

[49] Klir (1972, p 1).

[50] Von Bertalanffy (1972, pp 21–2).

[51] Von Bertalanffy (1972, p 23).

[52] Von Bertalanffy (1968, p 196).

[53] Ibid.

[54] Ray (2019, pp 27–8).

[55] Benjamin (2019, pp 11–12).

[56] Hanchard (1999, p 253).

[57] Hughey et al (2015, p 1350).

58 Hedström and Ylikoski (2010).
59 Hughey et al (2015, p 1350).
60 Meer (2012).
61 Hughey et al (2015).
62 Feagin (2001); (2006).
63 Feagin (2006, pp 25–6).
64 Meer (2014b).
65 Bauman (1989).
66 Meer (2020a).
67 Feagin and Elias (2013, p 936).
68 Du Bois (2007 [1920]).
69 Du Bois (2007 [1920], p 15).
70 Du Bois (2007 [1920], p 25).
71 See, for example, Lake and Reynolds (2008); Geary et al (2020).
72 Seamster and Ray (2018, p 326).
73 Winant (2001a, p 100).
74 Ignatiev (1995, p 1).
75 Ignatiev (1995, pp 2–3).
76 Palmer (2000).
77 Palmer (1998, p 91), emphasis added.
78 Burton (1997, p 232).
79 Mitchell (1991).
80 Ignatiev (1995), Palmer (1998) and Virdee (2014).
81 Palmer (1998, p 99).
82 Virdee (2014).
83 Virdee (2014, p 54).
84 Virdee (2014, p 64).
85 Du Bois (1971, p 416).
86 Du Bois (1935).
87 Dyre (1988).
88 Bhopal (2018).
89 Apata (2020, p 249).
90 Mills (2007, p 247).
91 Meer (2020b).
92 Ray (2019, p 35).
93 Brown (2006, p 142).
94 Wood (2020).
95 Ladson-Billings (1998, p 7).
96 Delgado (1995, p xiv).
97 Ibid.
98 Essed (1991).
99 Ahmed (2010)
100 Goldberg (2006, p 339).
101 Hall (2017).
102 Hall (2017, p 45).
103 Smith (2010).

104 Meer (2013a).
105 Crenshaw et al (1995, p xiv).
106 Ladson-Billings (1998, p 15).
107 Preston and Chadderton (2012).
108 Feagin and Elias (2013, p 938).
109 Feagin and Elias (2013, p 951).
110 Jones (1969 [1925], p 41).
111 Williams (2003, p 208).
112 Honig (2013, p 17).
113 Meer (2012).
114 Mills (1959, p 226).
115 Parekh (2000).
116 Williams and Mohammed (2013).
117 Marmot (2020, p 23).
118 Phelan and Link (2015).
119 IOM (2015).
120 Meer and Villegas (2020).
121 Elia (2013, p 36).
122 Omi and Winant (2009, pp 124–5).
123 Mondon and Winter (2020).

Chapter Two

1 Béland and Lecours (2005, p 679).
2 Bevir and Rhodes (2003).
3 Gilroy (1990, p 119).
4 Burton (1997, p 234).
5 Ibid.
6 Du Bois (2007 [1920], p 18).
7 Moses (2002, p 33).
8 Stoler (1995, p 9).
9 Balibar and Wallerstein (1991, p 2).
10 Miles (1987, p 27).
11 CMEB (2000).
12 Hall (1980).
13 Bauman (1995, p 22)
14 Hall (1992).
15 Hawthorne (2004, p 99).
16 Calhoun (1994), quoted in Sicakkan and Lithman (2005, p 3).
17 Hall (1992, pp 275–6).
18 Brubaker and Cooper (2000, p 1).
19 Guttman (2003, p 2).
20 Young (1995, p 187).
21 Ibid.
22 Meer (2014b).
23 McCarthy (2004, p 768).
24 Sicakkan and Lithman (2005, p 2).

[25] Feagin and Elias (2013, p 937).

[26] Agamben (1998, p 95).

[27] De Genova (2017, p 1766).

[28] Agamben (1998).

[29] De Genova (2017, p 1766).

[30] Goldberg (2002).

[31] Anderson (1991).

[32] Anderson (1991, p 6).

[33] Bhabha (1990, p 293).

[34] Schwarz (1986, p 155).

[35] Butler (2015, p 78).

[36] Hanchard (1999, p 253).

[37] Hanchard (1999, p 257).

[38] Connell (2007); cf Meer (2017).

[39] Mazower (1994, p 5).

[40] Hanchard (1999, p 257).

[41] Ibid.

[42] Kaviraj (1993).

[43] Burton (1997, p 240).

[44] Gellner (2008), p 42. Naturally, nationalism scholars in the Global South have obviously taken much more interest in how race and Empire were integral to European nationalism. This only further goes to prove the point.

[45] Seeley (1971 [1883]), p 12.

[46] Hartman (2007, p 6).

[47] Hobsbawm (1968).

[48] Williams (1944).

[49] Without wishing to rehearse textbook definitions that are abundant elsewhere, different readings of the provenance of nations and nationalism are typically narrated either as comprising 'primarily a political principle, which holds that the political and national unit should be congruent' (Gellner, 1983, p 35), or that the nation is made up of a 'self-defining human community whose members cultivate shared memories, symbols, myths, traditions and values, inhabit and are attached to historic territories or "homelands", create and disseminate a distinctive public culture, and observe shared customs and standardised laws' (Smith, 2009, p 29). Inevitably, these 'poles' are not always as distant from one another as is sometimes claimed.

[50] Anderson (1991 [1983], p 149).

[51] Moses (2002, p 54).

[52] Berman (1982).

[53] cf Césaire (2001).

[54] cf Lugard (1922).

[55] Bales (1999); Blackburn (1997).

[56] Hall (1980, p 338).

[57] Moses (2002, p 34).

[58] Wolfe (2016, p 11).

[59] McCarthy (2004, p 769).
[60] Venn (2003, p 3).
[61] Ibid.
[62] Meer (2013a; 2018b).
[63] Bhambra (2015).
[64] For example, Meer (2010).
[65] Bhambra (2017, p 402).
[66] Tudor (2018).
[67] Vernon (2020).
[68] Referred to by Wendy Williams (2020: 8) in her *Independent* review.
[69] NAO (2018).
[70] Orwell (1949).
[71] Valluvan (2017).
[72] Leddy-Owen (2019).
[73] Wekker (2016).
[74] Banton (1955); (1959); (1967).
[75] Glass (1960).
[76] Patterson (1965); (1969).
[77] Rex and Moore (1979 [1967]).
[78] Rose (1969).
[79] Park (1950, p 82).
[80] Banton (1967).
[81] Zubaida (1972, p 141).
[82] Rex (1973).
[83] Solomos (1993, p 22).
[84] Miles, quoted in Ashe and McGeever (2011, p 2017).
[85] Miles (1988, p 438).
[86] Gilroy (1987, p 23).
[87] Hall (1999, p 191).
[88] Hall (1991); (1996 [1988]).
[89] Modood (1992).
[90] Ibid.
[91] Ibid, p 48.
[92] Cohen (2000), p 5.
[93] Alibhai-Brown (2001, p 47).
[94] Hall (2000).
[95] CMEB (2000, p viii).
[96] CMEB (2000, p 296).
[97] CMEB (2000, p 297).
[98] CMEB (2000, p 296).
[99] Uberoi (2015).
[100] Hall (1978, p 26).
[101] Olusoga (2018)
[102] Hartman (1997, p 31).
[103] Dahlgreen (2016).
[104] Gilroy (2006, p 5).

[105] Bowen (2006).
[106] Johnston (2000).
[107] McCarthy (2004, pp 757–8).
[108] CMEB (2000).
[109] Lester (2003).
[110] Uberoi and Modood (2013); Levey (2019).
[111] Meer (2015).
[112] Baldwin (1998, p 333).
[113] Gilroy (1982, p 278).
[114] Lawrence (1982 [2005], p 47).
[115] Department for Education (2015).
[116] Ibid.
[117] Mosse (1995, p 167).
[118] Home Office (2011).
[119] Young (1990, p 165).
[120] Billig (1995).
[121] Billig (2009, p 349).
[122] Gellner (1983, p 130).
[123] May (2001, p 61).
[124] Feagin and Elias (2013, p 945).
[125] Baldwin (1998, p 723).

Chapter Three

[1] Lewis (1996, p 34).
[2] https://www.toqonline.com/archives/v1n1/TOQv1n1Powell.pdf
[3] Meer (2018c).
[4] The text of the speech is available at https://www.toqonline.com/archives/v1n1/TOQv1n1Powell.pdf
[5] *Hansard*, Cmnd 6234, September 1976, para 13.
[6] Steel (1968, p 156).
[7] Quoted in Steel (1968, p 165).
[8] Cabinet Office (2017).
[9] Cabinet Office (2017, paras 2.9, 5.12–5.13).
[10] Achiume (2018, p 9).
[11] Department for Work and Pensions (2020).
[12] ONS (2021) 'UK government ethnicity facts and figures, unemployment', https://www.ethnicity-facts-figures.service.gov.uk/work-pay-and-benefits/unemployment-and-economic-inactivity/unemployment/latest
[13] EHRC (2016b).
[14] TUC (2012, p 6).
[15] Bowyer et al (2020).
[16] Zwysen et al (2020).
[17] Ibid.
[18] Daniel (1968).
[19] Smith (1976); Brown (1984).
[20] ECU (2016).

21 Rollock (2019, p 25).
22 Mahtani (2014).
23 JRF (2017, p 26).
24 EHRC (2016a, p 27).
25 Achiume (2018, p 7).
26 Ministry of Housing, Communities and Local Government (2018).
27 Department of Education (2020).
28 Lammy (2017, p 3).
29 EHRC (2016b).
30 Lammy (2017, p 3).
31 Joseph-Salisbury et al (2020, p 23).
32 Wood et al (2009).
33 Zwysen et al (2020).
34 Zwysen et al (2020, p 9).
35 Kline et al (2021).
36 Ibid.
37 Reay (2018).
38 Aranda (2019).
39 Karlsen et al (2020, p 18).
40 O'Leary (2006).
41 Kenny (2004, p 32).
42 Dworkin (1978).
43 King (2010, p 96).
44 King (2010, p 95).
45 Mills (2018, p 79).
46 Scott (1999).
47 Scott (1999, p 4).
48 Scott (1999, p 3).
49 Scott (1999, p 4).
50 Meer (2008).
51 Beaman (2017).
52 Mills (2020, p 54).
53 Rudiger (2007).
54 Modood (2005); (2007).
55 Scott (1999, p 8).
56 CRED (2021), quoting Gillborn (2008).
57 Quoted in Minow (1997, p 56).
58 Modood (2005).
59 Mills (2018, p 83).
60 Parekh (2005, p 199).
61 Parekh (2005, p 200).
62 Ibid.
63 Fraser and Honneth (2004).
64 Fraser (1997, p 16).
65 Fraser (1997, p 23).
66 For example, Rawls (1999 [1971]).

67 Parekh (2005, p 207).
68 Wang (2018, p 286).
69 Macpherson (1999, para 6.34).
70 For a comprehensive account, see Mayberry (2008).
71 House of Commons and House of Lords Joint Committee on Human Rights (2020, p 16, para 40).
72 House of Commons and House of Lords Joint Committee on Human Rights (2020, p 16, para 42).
73 Ahmed (2012, p 38).
74 Ibid.
75 Macpherson (1999, para 2.17).
76 Scarman Report (1981, p 135).
77 Scarman Report (1981, p 110).
78 Williams (2020, p 7).
79 Dodd (2020).
80 Quoted in House of Commons and House of Lords Joint Committee on Human Rights (2020, p 13).
81 House of Commons and House of Lords Joint Committee on Human Rights (2020, p 4).
82 Meer (2010).
83 Macpherson (1999, para 6.48).
84 Department of Education (2020).
85 House of Commons and House of Lords Joint Committee on Human Rights (2020, p 21).
86 Sewell (2016, p 404).
87 Smith et al (2007).
88 CRED (2021, p 30).
89 CRED (2021, p 8).
90 CRED (2021, p 11).
91 Sewell (2009, p 55).
92 CRED (2021, p 41).
93 Summary of responses to the call for evidence: https://www.gov.uk/government/consultations/ethnic-disparities-and-inequality-in-the-uk-call-for-evidence/public-feedback/summary-of-responses-to-the-call-for-evidence#responses-to-question-6-reasons-for-health-inequalities
94 CRED (2021, p 41).
95 Bonilla-Silva (2014, p 174).
96 Mohdin (2021).
97 Vickerman (2013, p 8).
98 Cho (2009, p 1596).
99 Syal (2021).
100 Quoted in Macpherson (1999, para 6.33).

Chapter Four

1 Williams and Mohammed (2013).
2 Marmot (2020, p 23).

3 Otu et al (2020).
4 Phelan and Link (2015).
5 Sirleaf (2021, p 88).
6 Krieger (2020, p 1620).
7 PHE (2020).
8 Rothchild (2020); Malone (2020); Johnson and Buford (2020); Blasco and Rodriguez Camacho (2020); Qureshi et al (2020).
9 Goldberg (2002, p 203).
10 Ray (2019).
11 Gumber and Gumber (2020).
12 Herrick (2020).
13 Chouhan and Nazroo (2020, p 76); Scottish Diabetes Data Group (2018).
14 Qureshi et al (2020).
15 Chouhan and Nazroo (2020, p 76).
16 Hill (2015).
17 Gilmore (2007, p 247).
18 Gravlee (2020, p 1).
19 Platt et al (1994).
20 Lindhorst et al (2007).
21 Keating et al (2003).
22 Mohammed et al (2006).
23 Gravlee (2009).
24 Geronimus (1992).
25 McEwen (1998), cited in Phelan and Link (2015, p 321).
26 Gravlee (2009), Geronimus (1992) and McEwen (1998); see also Lindhorst et al (2007) and Savoca et al (2009).
27 Keating et al (2003).
28 Sharply (2001, p 66).
29 Gillam et al (1989).
30 Nazroo (1998).
31 Karlsen and Nazroo (2006, p 26).
32 Chaturvedi (2001).
33 Braun (2014).
34 See, e.g., Bradby (2003).
35 Karlsen and Nazroo (2006, p 26).
36 E.g. Chaturvedi (2001).
37 Davey Smith et al (2000).
38 Gravlee (2020, p 1).
39 Gilmore (2021).
40 Krieger (2020, p 1621).
41 Phelan and Link (2015, p 321).
42 Hill (2015).
43 Salway et al (2020).
44 Haque (2020).
45 Clark and Shankley (2020).
46 Lawrence (2020).

47 Siddique (2020).
48 Houlihan et al (2020); Nguyen et al (2020); Otu et al (2020); Shields et al (2020).
49 Nagpaul (2020); Ford (2020); Younis (2020).
50 Otu et al (2020); Hussein et al (2020); Nguyen et al (2020).
51 Qureshi et al (2014); Qureshi (2019).
52 TUC (2019).
53 Liebman et al (2020, p 332).
54 Clark and Shankley (2020).
55 Hall et al (2017, p 47).
56 Clark and Shankley (2020, p 14).
57 Clark and Shankley (2020); UK Government (2018).
58 Liebman et al (2020, p 333), quoting Salvage Editorial Collective (2020).
59 Washington (2007, p 33).
60 Curry (2020); Kapilashrami and Bhui (2020).

Chapter Five
1 Du Bois (1984 [1940], p 133).
2 Agamben (1998).
3 De Genova (2017, p 1768).
4 Goldberg (2002); (2006).
5 Butler (2004, p 30).
6 Goldberg (2002, p 43).
7 IOM (2015).
8 Meer and Villegas (2020).
9 Fassin (2011).
10 Meer et al (2021).
11 Lefebvre (1996, p 158).
12 Meer et al (2021).
13 Vandevoordt (2019, p 48).
14 Filomeno (2019, p 7).
15 Stone (2018, p 103).
16 Bauman (2003).
17 Bauman (2003, pp 5–6).
18 Evans and Bauman (2016).
19 Weber (1922).
20 Davis (1955).
21 Weber (1922, p 1213).
22 This includes, firstly, an obviously sociological interest in how 'the city is a settlement of closely spaced dwellings which form a colony so extensive that the reciprocal personal acquaintance of the inhabitants, elsewhere characteristic of the neighbourhood, is lacking' (Weber, 1922, p 1212), precisely the concern with anonymity that so interested Simmel. Secondly, role of the 'market center' of the city, either as an industrial, merchant or service base, or, today, an economy reliant on consumption or production, or a combination therein (Weber, 1922, pp 1215–17). And thirdly, the

administrative and legal dimension of city as a corporate body with a given territory. This latter point continues be as relevant as the first two, and in a way that reminds us that 'city-generating factors' remains a useful heuristic device, a cluster of ideal types indeed, that need a contemporary – rather than medieval – focus.

23 Sassen (1991).
24 Massey (2007).
25 Glick Schiller (2015, p 2279).
26 Hill et al (2021).
27 Barber (2013).
28 Back and Sinha (2018).
29 Hall (2010).
30 Kloosterman (2019).
31 Albertsen and Diken (2004).
32 Borkert and Caponio (2010, p 19); cf de Graauw and Vermeulen (2016).
33 Elia (2013), p 36.
34 Following Brah (1996).
35 Phillips (2006), p 539.
36 Wacquant (1998).
37 To borrow from Agamben (2005).
38 See Bhambra (2015), (2017); Mayblin (2017) and El-Enany (2020).
39 Mayblin (2017).
40 Achiume (2019).
41 El-Enany (2020, p 4).
42 Yuval-Davis et al (2018).
43 Hill et al (2021); Cheshire and Zappia (2016).
44 Harvey (2003).
45 Kos et al (2016, p 354).
46 Enshrined in Article 33 of the 1951 Refugee Convention, this principle insists that 'No Contracting State shall expel or return ('*refouler*') a refugee in any manner whatsoever to the frontiers of territories where his [or her] life or freedom would be threatened on account of his [or her] race, religion, nationality, membership of a particular social group or political opinion' (UNHCR, 1951).
47 As reported by France 24 (2020).
48 Tondo (2020).
49 Trilling (2020).
50 Zerka (2020).
51 Ashford (2020).
52 Meer and Villegas (2020).
53 UNHCR (2020a).
54 Fundamental Rights Agency (2020).
55 UNHCR (2020b).
56 Ambrosini (2017, p 597).
57 Haselbacher (2019, p 75).
58 Brenner (2004).

59   Myrberg (2017, p 324).
60   Wachsmuth (2012).
61   Emilsson (2015, p 4).
62   Filomeno (2017, p 11).

Chapter Six

1   Bangstad (2014).
2   Benjamin (1968).
3   Benjamin (1968, p 257).
4   Benjamin (1968, pp 257–8).
5   Anders Behring Breivik's Complete Manifesto '2083 – A European Declaration of Independence' (2011) is archived on Public Intelligence: https://publicintelligence.net/anders-behring-breiviks-complete-manifesto-2083-a-european-declaration-of-independence/ (accessed 24 January 2021).
6   Benjamin (1968, pp 257–8).
7   Meer (2006; 2012; 2013a; 2013b; 2014a; 2014c); Meer and Noorani (2008); Meer and Modood (2009); Meer et al (2010); Jansen and Meer (2020).
8   Eddy (2020).
9   'The Global Terrorism Database (GTD) is an open-source database including information on terrorist events around the world since 1970 (currently updated through 2018). Unlike many other event databases, the GTD includes systematic data on international as well as domestic terrorist incidents that have occurred during this time period and now includes over 190,000 cases. For each GTD incident, information is available on the date and location of the incident, the weapons used and nature of the target, the number of casualties, and – when identifiable – the identity of the perpetrator.' See https://www.start.umd.edu/data-tools/global-terrorism-database-gtd (accessed 7 January 2021).
10   Hage (2019).
11   Specia (2019).
12   BBC News (2019).
13   Sky News (2011).
14   APB News Bureau (2020).
15   Meer (2020a).
16   Ibid.
17   Ibid.
18   Camus (2012).
19   Mondon and Winter (2020).
20   Judt (2014).
21   Dyre (1988, p 44).
22   Mills (2020, p 36).
23   Du Bois (1935).
24   McIntosh (1988).
25   Mills (2015, p 219).

26 Eddo-Lodge (2018).
27 Lorde (1984, p 115).
28 Duster (2001, pp 114–15).
29 Du Bois (1999 [1920], p 148).
30 Solomos and Back (1994, p 143).
31 Hesse (2004, p 14).
32 Ibid.
33 Twine and Gallagher (2008, p 10).
34 Ignatiev (1995).
35 Blumenbach (1969).
36 Ani (1994).
37 Hartman (2008, pp 2–3).
38 Lorde (1984, p 207).
39 Davis (2002).
40 Jansen and Meer (2020).
41 Jennings (2010).
42 Jennings (2010, p 22).
43 Jansen and Meer (2020).
44 Meer (2014a).
45 Meer (2013b).
46 Thomas (2010).
47 Omi and Winant (1986, p 61).
48 Ibid.
49 Quijano (2000, p 533).
50 Mignolo (2009, p 19).
51 Gilroy (2004, p 56).
52 Gilroy (1993).
53 Gilroy (2004, p 58).
54 Matar (2009, p 217).
55 Drakulic (2009, p 234).
56 Winant (2001b, p 21).
57 See Hund (2006); Isaac (2004).
58 Mills (2011, p 61).
59 Thomas (2010, p 1747).
60 Matar (1999), (2009); Shapiro (1996).
61 Matar (2009), p 219.
62 Shapiro (2000), p 128.
63 Goldberg (2009, p 1280).
64 Kidd (1894); (1902).
65 See Meer (2012).
66 Camus (2012).
67 Steyn (2006a).
68 Steyn (2006b).
69 Ibid.
70 Amis, quoted in Dougary (2006).
71 Meer (2010).

72 Mills (1959, p 226).
73 Miles (1989, p 75).
74 Kaufmann (2018).

Chapter Seven

1 Lewis (1973); Reichenbach (1976); Kvart (1986); Pavel (1986).
2 Berlant (2011, pp 121–2).
3 Levitas (2013).
4 Collingwood (2013, p 97).
5 Dawson (2019).
6 Berlant (2011).
7 Du Bois (1999 [1920], pp 10–11).
8 Leverett Brown et al (2019).
9 Berlant (2011, p 10).
10 Ibid.
11 Feagin (2001), (2006).
12 Feagin and Elias (2013, p 951).
13 https://www.theroot.com/dr-martin-luther-king-jr-my-dream-has-turned-into-a-1791257458
14 Liebman et al (2020, p 332).
15 Milsum (1968, p 178).
16 Shulman (2011, p 143).
17 Glick Schiller (2015, p 2279).
18 Gilmore (2007, p 247).
19 Palmer (1998, p 91), emphasis added.
20 Burton (1997, p 232).
21 McCarthy (2004, p 769).
22 Mercuse (1968, p 143).
23 Bell (2020, p 394).
24 Benjamin (1968).
25 West (1989, p 229).
26 Steiner (1961, p 6).
27 West (1989).
28 Doyle (2011, p 20).
29 Back (2020, p 5).
30 Ibid.
31 Lorde (1984, p 123).

References

Achiume, T. (2018) 'End of mission statement of the Special Rapporteur on Contemporary Forms of Racism, Racial Discrimination, Xenophobia and Related Intolerance at the conclusion of her mission to the United Kingdom of Great Britain and Northern Ireland', United Nations Human Rights, Office of the High Commissioner, www.ohchr.org/EN/NewsEvents/Pages/DisplayNews.aspx?NewsID=23073&LangID=E

Achiume, E.T. (2019) 'Migration as decolonization', *Stanford Law Review*, 71, 1509. Available at SSRN: https://ssrn.com/abstract=3330353

Agamben, G. (1998) *Homo Sacer: Sovereign Power and Bare Life*, Stanford: Stanford University Press.

Agamben G. (2005) *State of Exception*, Chicago, IL: University of Chicago Press.

Ahmed, S. (2004) 'Affective economies', *Social Text*, 22(2), 117–39.

Ahmed, S. (2010) 'Feminist killjoys (and other willful subjects)', The Scholar and Feminist Online, The Barnard Center for Research on Women, http://sfonline.barnard.edu/polyphonic/print_ahmed.htm

Ahmed, S. (2012) *On Being Included: Racism and Diversity in Institutional Life*, Durham and London, NC: Duke University Press.

Albertsen, N. and Diken, B. (2004) 'Welfare and the city', *Nordisk Arkitekturforskning*, 17(2), 7–22, http://arkitekturforskning.net/na/article/view/235/197

Alibhai-Brown, Y. (2001) 'After multiculturalism', *The Political Quarterly,* 47–55.

Allen, K. (2017) 'BME career progression "could add £24bn a year to UK economy"', *The Guardian*, 28 February, https://www.theguardian.com/money/2017/feb/28/bme-career-progression-could-add-24bn-a-year-to-uk-economy

Ambrosini, M. (2017) 'Superdiversity, multiculturalism and local policies: A study on European cities', *Policy & Politics*, 45(4), 585–603.

Anderson, B. (1991) *Imagined Communities: Reflections on the Origin and Spread of Nationalism*, 2nd edn, London: Verso.

Ani, M. (1994) *Yurugu: An Afrikan-centered Critique of European Cultural Thought and Behaviour*. Trenton: Africa World Press, 1994.

Apata, G.O. (2020) '"I can't breathe": The suffocating nature of racism', *Theory, Culture & Society*, 37(7–8), 241–54.

APB News Bureau (2020) 'Christchurch shooting: Gunman Brenton Tarrant who massacred 51 worshippers sentenced to life without parole', updated 27 August, https://news.abplive.com/news/world/christchurch-mosque-shooting-gunman-brenton-tarrant-sentenced-to-life-without-parole-1322714

Aranda, C.L. (2019) 'Housing discrimination in America: Lessons from the last decade of paired-testing research', Stakeholder Perspectives: Fair Housing, https://www.urban.org/sites/default/files/publication/99836/housing_discrimination_in_america_-_claudia_aranda.pdf

Ashe, S.D. and McGeever, B.F. (2011) 'Marxism, racism and the construction of "race" as a social and political relation: An interview with Professor Robert Miles', *Ethnic and Racial Studies*, 34(12), 2009–26.

Ashford, J. (2020) 'How populists are exploiting the spread of coronavirus', *The Week*, 27 February.

Back, L. (2020) 'Hope's work', *Antipode*, 53(1), 3–20, doi.org/10.1111/anti.12644

Back, L. and Sinha, S. (2018) *Migrant City*, Routledge.

Bailey, N. and Sigona, N. (2020) 'Black Lives Matter: Is This a Turning Point?', IRiS: https://superdiversity.net/2020/09/04/black-lives-matter-is-this-a-turning-point/

Baldwin, J. (1962) 'To speak out about the world as it is, says James Baldwin, is the writer's job as much of the truth as one can bear', *The New York Times*, 14 January, Book Review, p BR11.

Baldwin, J. (1998) *Collected essays*, New York, NY: Library of America.

Bales, K. (1999) *Disposable People: New Slavery in the Global Economy*, Berkeley, CA: University of California Press.

Balibar, E. and Wallerstein, I. (1991) *Race, Nation, Class: Ambiguous Identities*, London: Verso.

Bangstad, S. (2014) *Anders Breivik and the Rise of Islamophobia*, London: Zed.

Banton, M. (1955) *The Coloured Quarter: Negro Immigrants in an English City*, London: Jonathan Cape.

Banton, M. (1959) *White and Coloured*, London: Jonathan Cape.

Banton, M. (1967) *Race Relations*. London: Tavistock.

Barber, B.R. (2013) *If Mayors Ruled the World: Dysfunctional Nations, Rising Cities*, New Haven, CT: Yale University Press.

Bargetz, B. (2015) 'The distribution of emotions: Affective politics of emancipation', *Hypatia* 30(3): 580–96.

Bauman, Z. (1989) *Modernity and the Holocaust*, Ithaca, NY: Cornell University Press.

Bauman, Z. (1995) *Life in Fragments: Essays in Postmodern Morality*, Oxford: Blackwell.

Bauman, Z. (2003) *City of Fears, City of Hopes*, London: Goldsmith's College.

BBC News (2019) 'San Diego synagogue attack suspect "evil"', says his family', 29 April, https://www.bbc.co.uk/news/world-us-canada-48096197

Beaman, J. (2017) *Citizen Outsider: Children of North African Immigrants in France*, Los Angeles, CA: University of California Press.

Béland, D. and Lecours, A. (2005) 'The politics of territorial solidarity: nationalism and social policy reform in Canada, the United Kingdom, and Belgium', *Comparative Political Studies*, 38(6), 676–703.

Bell, D. (2020) *Dreamworlds of Race: Empire and the Utopian Destiny of Anglo-America*, Princeton, NJ: Princeton University Press.

Benjamin, R. (2019) *Captivating Technology*, Durham, NC: Duke University Press.

Benjamin, W. (1968) *Theses on the Philosophy of History* (edited, with an introduction by Hannah Arendt), New York: Schocken Books.

Berlant, L. (2011) *Cruel Optimism*, Durham, NC: Duke University Press.

Berman, M. (1982) *All that is Solid Melts into Air: The Experience of Modernity*, New York: Simon & Schuster.

Bevir, M. and Rhodes, R. (2003) *Interpreting British Governance*, London: Routledge.

Bhabha, H. (ed) (1990) *Narrating the Nation*, London: Routledge.

Bhambra, G.K. (2015) 'Citizens and others: The constitution of citizenship through exclusion', *Alternatives*, 40(2), 102–14.

Bhambra, G.K. (2017) 'The current crisis of Europe: Refugees, colonialism, and the limits of cosmopolitanism', *European Law Journal*, 23(5), 395–405.

Bhopal, K. (2018) *White Privilege: The Myth of a Post-Racial Society*, Bristol: Policy Press.

Billig, M. (1995) *Banal Nationalism*, London: SAGE.

Billig, M. (2009) 'Reflecting on a critical engagement with banal nationalism: Reply to Skey', *The Sociological Review*, 57(2), 347–52.

Blackburn, R. (1997) *The Making of New World Slavery: From the Baroque to the Modern, 1492–1800*, London: Verso.

Blasco, P.G. and Rodriguez Camacho, M.F. (2020) 'COVID-19 and its impact on the Roma community: The case of Spain', *Somatosphere*, 31 March.

Blumenbach, J.F. (1969) *On the Natural Varieties of Mankind*, New York: Bergman Publishers.

Bonilla-Silva, E. (1997) 'Rethinking racism: Toward a structural interpretation', *American Sociological Review*, 62, 465–80.

Bonilla-Silva, E. (2014) *Racism without Racists: Color-Blind Racism and the Persistence of Racial Inequality in America*, 4th edn, New York: Roman and Littlefield.

Borkert, M. and Caponio, T. (2010) 'Introduction', in T. Caponio and M. Borkert (eds), *The local dimension of migration policymaking*, Amsterdam: Amsterdam University Press.

Bowcott, O. and Dodd, V. (2017) 'Exposed: "racial bias" in England and Wales criminal justice system', *The Guardian*, 8 September, https://www.theguardian.com/law/2017/sep/08/racial-bias-uk-criminal-justice-david-lammy

Bowen, J. (2006) *Why the French Don't Like Headscarves: Islam, the State and Public Space*, Princeton, NJ: Princeton University Press.

Bowyer, G., Henderson, M., White, D. and Wooley, S. (2020) *Race Inequality in the Workforce*, London: Carnegie UK Trust, UCL Centre for Longitudinal Studies and Operation Black Vote, https://cls.ucl.ac.uk/wp-content/uploads/2017/02/Race-Inequality-in-the-Workforce-Final.pdf

Bradby, H. (2003) 'Describing ethnicity in health research', *Ethnicity & Health*, 8(1), 5–13.

Brah, A. (1996) *Cartographies of Diaspora*, London: Routledge.

Braun, L. (2014) *Breathing Race into the Machine: The Surprising Career of the Spirometer from Plantation to Genetics*, Minneapolis: University of Minnesota Press.

Brenner, N. (2004) *New State Spaces: Urban Governance and the Rescaling of Statehood*, Oxford: Oxford University Press.

Brown, C. (1984) *Black and White Britain*, London: Heinemann.

Brown, W. (2006) *Regulating Aversion*, Oxford: Princeton University Press.

Brubaker, R. and Cooper, F. (2000) 'Beyond identity', *Theory and Society*, 29(1), 1–47.

Burton, A. (1997) 'Who needs the nation? Interrogating "British" history', *Journal of Historical Sociology*, 10(3), 227–48.

Butler, J. (2004) *Precarious Life: The Powers of Mourning and Violence*, London: Verso Books.

Butler, J. (2015) *Notes Toward a Performative Theory of Assembly*, Cambridge, MA: Harvard University Press.

Cabinet Office (2017) 'Race disparity audit: Summary findings from the ethnicity facts and figures website', www.ethnicity-facts-figures.service.gov.uk/static/race-disparity-audit-summary-findings.pdf

Calhoun, C. (1994) *Social Theory and the Politics of Identity*, Oxford: Blackwell.

Camus, R. (2012) *Le Grand Remplacement*, Paris: Chez l'auteur.

Césaire, A. (2001) *Discourse on Colonialism*, New York: Monthly Review.

Chaturvedi, N. (2001) 'Ethnicity as an epidemiological determinant – crudely racist or crucially important?', *International Journal of Epidemiology*, 30(5), 925–7.

Cheshire, L. and Zappia, G. (2016) 'Destination dumping ground: The convergence of "unwanted" populations in disadvantaged city areas', *Urban Studies*, 53(10), 2081–98.

Cho, S. (2009) 'Post-racialism', *Iowa Law Review*, 94(5), 1589–650.

Chouhan, K. and Nazroo, J. (2020) 'Health inequalities', in B. Byrne, C. Alexander, O. Khan, J. Nazroo and W. Shankley (eds), *Race and Inequality in the UK: State of the Nation*, Bristol: Policy Press.

Clark, K. and Shankley, W. (2020) 'Ethnic minorities in the labour market', in B. Byrne, C. Alexander, O. Khan, J. Nazroo and W. Shankley (eds), *Race and Inequality in the UK: State of the Nation*, Bristol: Policy Press, 127–48.

CMEB (Commission on the Future of Multi-Ethnic Britain) (2000) *The Future of Multi-Ethnic Britain*, London: Runnymede Trust/Profile Books.

Cohen, P. (2000) *New Ethnicities, Old Racisms*, London: Zed Books.

Cohn, N. and Quealy, K. (2020) 'How public opinion has moved on Black Lives Matter', *The New York Times*, https://www.nytimes.com/interactive/2020/06/10/upshot/black-lives-matter-attitudes.html

Collingwood, R.G. (2013) *R.G. Collingwood: An Autobiography and Other Writings: With Essays on Collingwood's Life and Work*, Oxford: Oxford University Press.

Connell, R. (2007) *Southern Social Theory: The Global Dynamics of Knowledge in Social Science*, Cambridge: Polity.

CRED (Commission on Race and Ethnic Disparities) (2021) *Commission on Race and Ethnic Disparities: The Report*, London: HMSO, p 8, https://assets.publishing.service.gov.uk/government/uploads/system/uploads/attachment_data/file/974507/20210331_-_CRED_Report_-_FINAL_-_Web_Accessible.pdf

Crenshaw, K., Gotanda, K., Peller, G. and Thomas, K. (eds) (1995) *Critical Race Theory: The Key Writings that Formed the Movement*, New York: The New York Press.

Curry, G. (2020) 'But they said we wouldn't find it here: Racism, discrimination, and COVID-19', *SCOPE*. https://blogs.ed.ac.uk/scope/2020/09/17/but-they-said-we-wouldnt-find-it-here-racism-discrimination-and-COVID-19/

Dahlgreen, W. (2016) 'Rhodes must not fall', https://yougov.co.uk/topics/politics/articles-reports/2016/01/18/rhodes-must-not-fall

Daniel, W.W. (1968) *Racial Discrimination in England*, Harmondsworth: Penguin.

Davey Smith, G., Chaturvedi, N., Harding, S., Nazroo, J. and Williams, R. (2000) 'Ethnic inequalities in health: a review of UK epidemiological evidence', *Critical Public Health*, 10(4): 375–408.

Davey Smith, G., Charsley, K. et al (2000) 'Ethnicity, health and the meaning of socioeconomic position', in H. Graham (ed.) *Understanding Inequalities in Health*, Buckingham: Open University Press.

Davis, K. (1955) 'Internal migration and urbanization in relation to economic development', *Proceedings of the World Population Conference, 1954*, New York: United Nations, 783–800.

Davis, M. (2002) *Late Victorian Holocausts: El Niño Famines and the Making of the Third World*, London: Verso Books.

Dawson, M. (2019) 'Retheorizing (racial) justice: A conversation with Charles Mills', https://www.raceandcapitalism.com/interviews-and-essays/retheorizing-racial-justice-a-conversation-with-charles-mills

De Genova, N. (ed) (2017) *The Borders of 'Europe': Autonomy of Migration, Tactics of Bordering*, Durham, NC: Duke University Press.

de Graauw, E. and Vermeulen, F. (2016) 'Cities and the politics of immigrant integration: a comparison of Berlin, Amsterdam, New York City, and San Francisco', *Journal of Ethnic and Migration Studies*, 42(6), 989–1012.

Department for Education (2015) *The Prevent Duty: Departmental Advice for Schools and Childcare Providers*, London: HMSO.

Department for Work and Pensions (2020) 'Persistent low income', https://www.ethnicity-facts-figures.service.gov.uk/work-pay-and-benefits/pay-and-income/low-income/latest

Department of Education (2020) 'Pupil exclusions: UK Government ethnicity facts and figures, pupil exclusions', https://www.ethnicity-facts-figures.service.gov.uk/education-skills-and-training/absence-and-exclusions/pupil-exclusions/latest

Delgado, R. (ed) (1995) *Critical Race Theory: The Cutting Edge*, Philadelphia: Temple University Press.

Dodd, V. (2017) 'Families of people who died in police custody failed by system – report', *The Guardian*, 4 September, https://www.theguardian.com/uk-news/2017/sep/04/families-of-people-who-died-in-police-custody-failed-by-system-report

Dodd, V. (2020) 'Met police officers investigated over black woman's assault claims', *The Guardian*, 24 November, https://www.theguardian.com/uk-news/2020/nov/24/met-police-officers-investigated-over-black-woman-assault-claims

Dougary, G. (2006) 'The voice of experience', *The Times*, 17 September.

Douglass, P., Terrefe, S.D. and Wilderson, F.B. (2018) 'Afro-Pessimism', in *African American Studies* (Oxford Bibliographies), ed G.A. Jarrett, p 1, doi:10.1093/obo/9780190280024-0056

Doyle, D. (2011) 'Changing hopes: The theological virtue of hope in Thomas Aquinas, John of the Cross, and Karl Rahner', *Irish Theological Quarterly*, 77(1), 18–36.

Drakulic, S. (2009) 'Anti-Turkish obsession and the exodus of Balkan Muslims', *Patterns of Prejudice*, 43(3–4), 233–50.

Du Bois, W.E.B. (1935) *Black Reconstruction: An Essay Toward a History of the Part Which Black Folk Played in the Attempt to Reconstruct Democracy in America, 1860–1880*, New York: Anteneum.

Du Bois, W.E.B. (1971) 'Does the Negro need separate schools?' in J. Lester (ed), *The Seventh Son: The Thought and Writings of W.E.B. Du Bois*, New York, NY: Random House, pp 408–18.

Du Bois, W.E.B. (1984 [1940]) *Dusk of Dawn: An Essay Toward an Autobiography of a Race Concept*, New Brunswick, NJ: Transaction.

Du Bois, W.E.B. (1999 [1903]) *The Souls of Black Folk*, Norton Critical Editions, eds H.L. Gates, and T.H. Oliver, New York, NY: Norton.

Du Bois, W.E.B. (1999 [1920]) *Darkwater: Voices From Within the Veil*, Mineola, NY: Dover.

Du Bois, W.E.B. (2007 [1920]) 'The souls of White folk', in *Darkwater: Voices from within the Veil*, New York: Washington Square Press.

Duster, T. (2001) 'The "morphing" of properties of whiteness', in B.B. Rasmussen, E. Klinenberg, I. Nexica and M. Wray (eds), *The Making and Unmaking of Whiteness*, Durham, NC: Duke University Press.

Dworkin, R. (1978) *Taking Rights Seriously*, Cambridge, MA: Harvard University Press.

Dyre, R. (1988) 'White', *Screen*, 29(4): 44–65, doi:10.1093/screen/29.4.44

ECU (Equality Challenge Unit) (2016) 'Equality in higher education: statistical report 2016', www.ecu.ac.uk/publications/equality-in-higher-education-statistical-report-2016/

Eddo-Lodge, R. (2018) *Why I'm No Longer Talking to White People About Race*, London: Bloomsbury Publishing.

Eddy, M. (2020) 'Far-Right terrorism is No. 1 threat, Germany is told after attack', *The New York Times*, 21 February, https://www.nytimes.com/2020/02/21/world/europe/germany-shooting-terrorism.html

EHRC (Equality and Human Rights Commission) (2016a) 'Is England fairer? The state of equality and human rights 2016'. Available at: https://www.equalityhumanrights.com/sites/default/files/is-england-fairer-2016.pdf

EHRC (2016b) 'Healing a divided Britain: The need for a comprehensive race equality strategy'. Available at: https://www.equalityhumanrights.com/sites/default/files/healing_a_divided_britain_-_the_need_for_a_comprehensive_race_equality_strategy_final.pdf

El-Enany, N. (2020) *(B)ordering Britain: Law, Race and Empire*, Manchester University Press.

Elia, A. (2013) 'The arrival of North African migrants in the south of Italy: practices of sustainable welfare within a nonwelcoming system', in E. Januszewska and S. Rullac (eds), *Social Problems in Europe: Dilemmas and Possible Solutions*, Paris: L'Harmattan.

Emilsson, E. (2015) 'A national turn of local integration policy: multilevel governance dynamics in Denmark and Sweden', *Comparative Migration Studies*, 3(7), 1–17.

Essed, P. (1991) *Understanding Everyday Racism: An Interdisciplinary Theory*, Amsterdam: University of Amsterdam.

Evans, B. and Bauman, Z. (2016) 'The refugee crisis is humanity's crisis', *The New York Times*, https://www.nytimes.com/2016/05/02/opinion/the-refugee-crisis-is-humanitys-crisis

Fanon, F. (1968) *The Wretched of the Earth*, New York: Grove Press.

Fassin, D. (2011) 'Policing borders, producing boundaries: The governmentality of immigration in dark times', *Annual Review of Anthropology*, 40(1): 213–26.

Feagin, J.R. (2001) *Racist America: Roots, Current Realities, and Future Reparations*, Psychology Press.

Feagin, J.R. (2006) *Systemic Racism: A Theory of Oppression*, New York: Routledge.

Feagin, J. and Elias, S. (2013) 'Rethinking racial formation theory: A systemic racism critique', *Ethnic and Racial Studies*, 36(6), 931–60.

Filomeno, F.A. (2017) *Theories of Local Immigration Policy*, Basingstoke: Palgrave.

Filomeno, F.A. (2019) 'The potential of dialogues on social identity and diversity for immigrant civic integration', *Evaluation and Program Planning*, 77, p 101723.

Ford, M. (2020) 'Exclusive: BME nurses "feel targeted" to work on COVID-19 wards', 17 April, https://www.nursingtimes.net/news/coronavirus/exclusive-bme-nurses-feel-targeted-to-work-on-covid-19-wards-17-04-2020/

France 24 (2020) 'Hungary's Orban blames foreigners, migration for coronavirus spread', 13 March. Available at: https://www.france24.com/en/20200313-hungary-s-pm-orban-blames-foreign-students-migration-for-coronavirus-spread

Fraser, N. (1997) *Justice Interruptus: Critical Reflections on the 'Postsocialist' Condition*, London: Verso.

Fraser, N. and Honneth, A. (2004) *Redistribution or Recognition? A Political–Philosophical Exchange*, London: Verso.

Fundamental Rights Agency (2020) *Migration: Key Fundamental Rights Concerns – Quarterly Bulletin 2*, Vienna: FRA, https://fra.europa.eu/en/publication/2020/migration-key-fundamental-rights-concerns-quarterly-bulletin-2-2020

Geary, G., Schofield, C. and Sutton, J. (eds) (2020) *Global White Nationalism: From Apartheid to Trump*, Manchester: Manchester University Press.

Gellner, E. (1983) *Nations and Nationalism*, Oxford: Basil Blackwell.

Gellner, E. (2008) *Nations and Nationalism*, Ithaca, NY: Cornell University Press.

Gentleman, A. (2020) 'Windrush review to call for reform of "reckless" Home Office'. *The Guardian*, 19 March, https://www.theguardian.com/uk-news/2020/mar/19/windrush-review-to-call-for-reform-of-reckless-home-office

Geronimus, A.T. (1992) 'The weathering hypothesis and the health of African-American women and infants: evidence and speculations', *Ethnicity & Disease*, 2(3): 207–21.

Gillam, S.J., Jarman, B., White, P. and Law, R. (1989) 'Ethnic differences in consultation rates in urban general practice', *BMJ*, 299(6705), 953–7.

Gillborn, D. (2008) *Racism in Education: Coincidence or Conspiracy?*, London: Routledge.

Gilmore, R.W. (2007) *Golden Gulag*, Berkeley, CA: University of California Press.

Gilmore, R.W. (2021) 'COVID-19, decarceration and abolition'. Available at https://www.haymarketbooks.org/blogs/128-ruth-wilson-gilmore-on-covid-19-decarceration-and-abolition

Gilroy, P. (1982) '"Steppin' out of Babylon" – race, class and autonomy', in Centre for Contemporary Cultural Studies (ed), *The Empire Strikes Back: Race and Racism in 70s Britain*, Birmingham: Hutchinson University Library, 276–315.

Gilroy, P. (1987) *'There Ain't No Black in the Union Jack': The Cultural Politics of Race and Nation*, London: Hutchinson.

Gilroy, P. (1990) 'Nationalism, history and ethnic absolutism', *History Workshop Journal*, 30(1), 114–20.

Gilroy, P. (1993) *Black Atlantic: Modernity and Double Consciousness*, London: Verso.

Gilroy, P. (2004) *Between Camps*, New York: Routledge.

Gilroy, P. (2006) 'Multiculture in times of war', Inaugural address to the LSE, https://onlinelibrary.wiley.com/doi/10.1111/j.1467-8705.2006.00731.x

Glass, R. (1960) *Newcomers: West Indians in London*, London: Allen and Unwin.

Glick Schiller, N. (2015) 'Explanatory frameworks in transnational migration studies: the missing multi-scalar global perspective', *Ethnic and Racial Studies*, 38(13), 2275–82.

Goldberg, D.T. (2002) *The Racial State*, Oxford: Blackwell.

Goldberg, D.T. (2006) 'Racial Europeanization', *Ethnic and Racial Studies*, 29(2), 332–64.

Goldberg, D. (2009) 'Racial comparisons, relational racisms: Some thoughts on method', *Ethnic and Racial Studies*, 32(7): 1271–82.

Gravlee, C.C. (2009) 'How race becomes biology: Embodiment of social inequality', *American Journal of Physical Anthropology*, 139(1): 47–57.

Gravlee, C.C. (2020) 'Systemic racism, chronic health inequities, and COVID-19: A syndemic in the making?', *American Journal of Human Biology*, 32(5), doi.org/10.1002/ajhb.23482

Gumber, A. and Gumber, L. (2020) 'Rapid Response to: "Is ethnicity linked to incidence or outcomes of COVID-19?"', *BMJ*, 369, m1548, https://www.bmj.com/content/369/bmj.m1548/rr-9

Guttman, A. (2003) *Identity and Democracy*, Princeton, NJ: Princeton University Press.

Hage, G. (2019) 'White entitlement is part of the very structure of Australian society', https://www.theguardian.com/commentisfree/2019/mar/18/white-entitlement-is-part-of-the-very-structure-of-australian-society

Hage, G. (2020) 'Intellectual anti-colonialism needs to offer an alternative ethics'. Available at: https://www.abc.net.au/religion/ghassan-hage-ethics-after-terror-attacks/12848046

Hall, S. (1978) 'Racism and reaction', in Commission for Racial Equality (CRE) (ed), *Five Views on Multiracial Britain*, London: CRE, 22–35.

Hall, S. (1980) 'Race, articulation and societies structured in dominance', in UNESCO (ed), *Sociological Theories: Race and Colonialism*, Paris: UNESCO, 305–45.

Hall, S. (1991) 'Old ethnicities, new ethnicities', in A.D. King (ed), *Culture, Globalization and the World System*, London: Macmillan.

Hall, S. (1992) 'The question of cultural identity', in S. Hall, D. Held and T. McGrew (eds), *Modernity and its Futures*, Cambridge: Polity Press, 274–314.

Hall, S. (1996 [1988]) 'New ethnicities', in H.A. Baker Jr, M. Diawara and R.H. Lindeborg (eds), *Black British Cultural Studies: A Reader*, Chicago: University of Chicago Press, 163–72.

Hall, S. (1999) 'Scarman to Stephen Lawrence', *History Workshop Journal*, 48, 187–97.

Hall, S. (2000) 'A question of identity (II)', *The Guardian*, 15 October, https://www.theguardian.com/uk/2000/oct/15/britishidentity.comment1

Hall, S. (2017) *Selected Political Writings: The Great Moving Right Show and Other Essays*, Books Gateway: Duke University Press (dukeupress.edu).

Hall, S.M. (2010) 'Picturing difference: Juxtaposition, collage and layering of a multiethnic street', *Anthropology Matters*, 12(1), 1–17.

Hall, S.-M., McIntosh, K., Neitzert, E., Pottinger, L., Sandhu, K., Stephenson, M.-A., Reed, H. and Taylor, L. (2017) 'Intersecting inequalities: the impact of austerity on Black and Minority Ethnic women in the UK', Women's Budget Group and the Runnymede Trust with Reclaim and Coventry Women's Voices, http://wbg.org.uk/wpcontent/uploads/2018/08/Intersecting-Inequalities-October-2017-Full-Report.pdf

Hanchard, M. (1999) 'Afro-Modernity: Temporality, politics, and the African diaspora', *Public Culture*, 11(1): 245–68.

Haque, Z. (2020) 'Coronavirus will increase race inequalities', Race Matters blog post, Runnymede Trust, 26 March, https://www.runnymedetrust.org/blog/coronavirus-will-increase-race-inequalities

Hartman, S.V. (1997) *Scenes of Subjection: Terror, Slavery, and Self-Making in Nineteenth-Century America*, Oxford: Oxford University Press.

Hartman, S. (2007) *Lose Your Mother: A Journey Along the Atlantic Slave Route*, New York: Farrar, Straus, and Giroux.

Hartman, S. (2008) 'Venus in Two Acts', *Small Axe*, 26, 1–14.

Harvey, D. (2003) *The New Imperialism*, Oxford: Oxford University Press.

Haselbacher, M. (2019) 'Solidarity as a field of political contention: Insights from local reception realities', *Social Inclusion*, 7(2), 74–84.

Hawthorne, J. (2004) 'Identity', in M.J. Loux and D.W. Zimmerman (eds), *The Oxford Handbook of Metaphysics*, Oxford: Oxford University Press.

Hedström, P. and Ylikoski, P. (2010) 'Causal mechanisms in the social sciences', *Annual Review of Sociology*, 36.

Herrick, C. (2020) 'Syndemics of COVID-19 and "preexisting conditions"', *Somatosphere*, 30 March, http://somatosphere. net/2020/syndemics-of-COVID-19-and-pre-existing-conditions.html/

Hesse, B. (2004) 'The im/plausible deniability: Racism's conceptual double bind', *Social Identities*, 10(1), 9–29.

Hill, S. (2015) 'Axes of health inequalities and intersectionality', in K. Smith, C. Bambra and S. Hill (eds), *Health Inequalities: Critical Perspectives*, Oxford: Oxford University Press.

Hill, E., Meer, N. and Peace, T. (2021) 'The role of asylum in processes of urban gentrification', *The Sociological Review*, p.0038026120970359.

Hobsbawm, E. (1968) *Industry and Empire: An Economic History of Britain since 1750*, London: Weidenfeld & Nicolson.

Holt, L.F. and Sweitzer, M.D. (2020) 'More than a black and white issue: Ethnic identity, social dominance orientation, and support for the black lives matter movement', *Self and Identity*, 19(1), 16–31.

Home Office (2011) *Prevent Strategy*, London: HMSO, https:// assets.publishing.service.gov.uk/government/uploads/system/ uploads/attachment_data/file/97976/prevent-strategy-review. pdf

Home Office (2021) *Home Office Measures in the Police, Crime, Sentencing and Courts Bill: Equalities Impact Assessment*, London: HMSO. Viewed online: https://www.gov.uk/government/ publications/police-crime-sentencing-and-courts-bill-2021-equality-statements/home-office-measures-in-the-police-crime-sentencing-and-courts-bill-equalities-impact-assessment

Honig, B. (2013) *Antigone, Interrupted*, Cambridge: New York: Cambridge University Press.

Houlihan, C., Vora, N., Byrne, T., Lewer, D. Heaney, J., Moore, D.A. et al (2020) 'SARS-CoV-2 virus and antibodies in front-line health care workers in an acute hospital in London: preliminary results from a longitudinal study', doi. org/10.1101/2020.06.08.20120584

House of Commons and House of Lords Joint Committee on Human Rights (2020) *Black People, Racism and Human Rights*, Eleventh Report of Session 2019–21, https://committees. parliament.uk/publications/3376/documents/32359/default/

Hughey, M.W., Embrick, D.G. and Doane, A.W. (2015) 'Paving the way for future race research: Exploring the racial mechanisms within a color-blind, racialized social system', *American Behavioral Scientist*, 59(11), 1347–57.

Hund, W.D. (2006) *Negative Vergesellschaftung: Dimensions der Rassismusanalyse*, Munster: Westfälisches Dampfboot.

Hussein, S., Saloniki, E., Turnpenny, A., Collins, G., Vadean, F., Bryson, A. et al (2020) *COVID-19 and the Wellbeing of the Adult Social Care Workforce: Evidence from the UK*, Canterbury: Personal Social Services Research Unit, University of Kent.

Ignatiev, M. (1995) *How the Irish Became White*, New York: Routledge.

IOM (International Organization for Migration) (2015) *Situation Report on International Migration: Migration Displacement and Development in a Changing Arab Region 2015*, United Nations and International Organization for Migration.

Isaac, B. (2004) *The Invention of Race in Classical Antiquity*, Princeton, NJ: Princeton University Press.

Jansen, Y. and Meer, N. (2020) 'Genealogies of "Jews" and "Muslims": Social imaginaries in the race–religion nexus', *Patterns of Prejudice*, 54(1–2), 1–14.

Jennings, W.J. (2010) *The Christian Imagination: Theology and the Origins of Race*, New Haven, CT: Yale University Press.

Johnson, A. and Buford, T. (2020) 'Early data shows African Americans have contracted and died of coronavirus at an alarming rate', *ProPublica*, 3 April.

Johnston, P. (2000) 'Straw wants to rewrite our history', *The Telegraph*, 10 October, https://www.telegraph.co.uk/news/uknews/1369663/Straw-wants-to-rewrite-our-history.html

Jones, M. (1969 [1925]) *Autobiography of Mother Jones*, reprint of 1925 edn, New York, NY: Arno Press, www.digital.library.upenn.edu/women/jones/autobiography/autobiograph.html

Joseph-Salisbury, R., Connelly, L.J. and Wangari-Jones, P. (2020) '"The UK is not innocent": Black Lives Matter, policing and abolition in the UK', *Equality, Diversity and Inclusion*, 40(1), 21–8.

JRF (Joseph Rowntree Foundation) (2017) *UK Poverty 2017: A Comprehensive Analysis of Poverty Trends and Figures*, London: JRF, www.jrf.org.uk/sites/default/files/jrf/files-research/uk_poverty_2017.pdf

Judt, T. (2014) *Reappraisals: Reflections on the Forgotten Twentieth Century*, London: Random House.

Kapilashrami, A. and Bhui, K. (2020) 'Mental health and COVID-19: Is the virus racist?', *The British Journal of Psychiatry*, 217(2), 405–7.

Karlsen, S. and Nazroo, J. (2006) 'Defining and measuring ethnicity and "race": theoretical conceptual issues for health and social care research', in J. Nazroo (ed), *Health and Social Research in Multiethnic Societies*, London: Routledge.

Karlsen, S., Nazroo, J. and Smith, N. (2020) 'Ethnic, religious and gender differences in intragenerational economic mobility in England and Wales', *Sociology*, 54(5), 883–903.

Kaufmann, E. (2018) *Whiteshift: Populism, Immigration and the Future of White Majorities*, Penguin UK.

Kaviraj, S. (1993) 'The imaginary institution of India', in P. Chatterjee and G. Pandey (eds), *Subaltern Studies VII: Writings on South Asian History and Society*, Delhi: Oxford University Press, pp 1–39.

Keating, M., Stevenson, L., Cairney, P. and Taylor, K. (2003) 'Does devolution make a difference? Legislative output and policy divergence in Scotland', *The Journal of Legislative Studies*, 9(3), 110–39.

Kenny, M. (2004) *The Politics of Identity*, Cambridge: Polity.

Kidd, B. (1894) *Social Evolution*, London: Macmillan.

Kidd, B. (1902) *Principles of Western Civilization*, London: Macmillan.

King, M.L. (2010) *Where Do We Go from Here?*, Boston: Beacon Books.

Kline, P.M., Rose, E.K. and Walters, C.R. (2021) 'Systemic discrimination among large US employers', https://www.nber.org/papers/w29053

Klir, G.J. (1972) 'The polyphonic general systems theory', in G.J. Klir (ed), *Trends in General Systems Theory*, New York: John Wiley & Sons, Inc, p 1.

Kloosterman, R.C. (2019) 'Migrant entrepreneurs and cities: New opportunities, newcomers, new issues', in T. Caponio, P. Scholten and R. Zapata-Barrero (eds), *The Routledge Handbook of the Governance of Migration and Diversity in Cities*, Abingdon: Routledge.

Kos, S., Maussen, M. and Doomernik, J. (2016) 'Policies of exclusion and practices of inclusion: How municipal governments negotiate asylum policies in the Netherlands', *Territory, Politics, Governance*, 4(3), 354–74.

Krieger, N. (2020) 'ENOUGH: COVID-19, structural racism, police brutality, plutocracy, climate change – and time for health justice, democratic governance, and an equitable, sustainable future', *American Journal of Public Health*, 110(11), 1620–3.

Kvart, I. (1986) *A Theory of Counterfactuals*, Indianapolis, IN: Hackett Pub. Co.

Ladson-Billings, G. (1998) 'Just what is critical race theory and what's it doing in a nice field like education?', *Qualitative Studies in Education*, 11(1), 7–24.

Lake, M. and Reynolds, H. (2008) *Drawing the Global Colour Line: White Men's Countries and the International Challenge of Racial Equality*, Critical Perspectives on Empire, Cambridge: Cambridge University Press, doi:10.1017/CBO9780511805363

Lammy, D. (2017) 'An independent review into the treatment of, and outcomes for, black, Asian and minority ethnic individuals in the criminal justice system', www.gov.uk/government/publications/lammy-review-final-report

Lawrence, D. (2020) 'An avoidable crisis', *Lawrence Review*, https://www.lawrencereview.co.uk/chapters/foreword

Lawrence, E. (1982 [2005]) 'In the abundance of water the fool is thirsty: Sociology and black "pathology"', in Centre for Contemporary Cultural Studies (ed), *The Empire Strikes Back: Race and Racism in 70s Britain*, Birmingham: Hutchinson University Library.

Leddy-Owen, C. (2019) *Nationalism, Inequality and England's Political Predicament*, London: Routledge.

Lefebvre, H. (1996) *Writings on Cities*, trs. E. Kofman and E. Lebas, Cambridge, MA: Blackwell.

Lester, A. (2003) 'Nailing the lie and promoting equality – The Jim Rose Lecture', Runnymede Trust, 15 October, http://www.runnymedetrust.org/uploads/events/aLesterSpeech.pdf

Leverett Brown, S., Johnson, Z. and Miller, S.E. (2019) 'Racial microaggressions and black social work students: A call to social work educators for proactive models informed by social justice', *Social Work Education*, 38(5), 618–30.

Levey, G. (2019) 'The Bristol School of Multiculturalism', *Ethnicities*, 19(1), 200–26.

Levitas, R. (2013) *Utopia as Method: The Imaginary Reconstitution of Society*, Palgrave Macmillan.

Lewis, D. (1973) *Counterfactuals*, Oxford: OUP.

Lewis, G. (1996) 'Situated voices: black women's experience and social work', *Feminist Review*, 53, 24–56.

Liebman, A., Rhiney, K. and Wallace, R. (2020) 'To die a thousand deaths: COVID-19, racial capitalism, and anti–Black violence', *Human Geography*, 13(3), 331–5.

Lindhorst, J., Alexander, N., Blignaut, J. and Rayner, B. (2007) 'Differences in hypertension between blacks and whites: an overview'. *Cardiovascular Journal of Africa*, 18(4), 241–7.

Logan, L. (2020) *Closing Ranks: My Life as a Cop*, London: SPCK Publishing.

Lorde, A. (1984) *Sister Outsider: Essays and Speeches*, Trumansburg, NY: The Crossing Press.

Lugard, F.D. (1922) *The Dual Mandate in British Tropical Africa*, Edinburgh: W. Blackwood and Sons.

Macpherson, Lord (1999) *The Stephen Lawrence Inquiry*, London: HMSO.

Mahtani, M. (2014) 'Toxic geographies: Absences in critical race thought and practice in social and cultural geography', *Social and Cultural Geography*, 15(4), 359–67.

Malone, C. (2020) 'New York's inequalities are fueling COVID-19', *FiveThirtyEight*, 10 April.

Marmot, M. (2020) 'Health equity in England: The Marmot Review 10 years on', *BMJ*, p.m693, doi.org/10.1136/bmj.m693

Massey, D. (2007) *World City*, Cambridge: Polity.

Matar, N. (1999) *Turks, Moors, and Englishmen in the Age of Discovery*, New York: Columbia University Press.

Matar, N. (2009) 'Britons and Muslims in the Early Modern period: From prejudice to (a theory of) toleration', *Patterns of Prejudice*, 43(3–4), 212–31.

May, S. (2001) *Language and Minority Rights: Ethnicity, Nationalism and the Politics of Language*, Malaysia CLP: Pearson Publishing.

Mayberry, D. (2008) *Black Death in Police Custody and Human Rights: The Failure of the Stephen Lawrence Inquiry*, London: Hansib.

Mayblin, L. (2017) *Asylum after Empire: Colonial Legacies in the Politics of Asylum Seeking*, London: Rowman & Littlefield International.

Mazower, M. (1994) 'After Lemkin: Genocide, the Holocaust and history', *Jewish Quarterly*, 5, 5–8.

McCarthy, T. (2004) 'Coming to terms with our past, Part II: On the morality and politics of reparations for slavery', *Political Theory*, 32(6), 750–72.

McEwen, B. (1998) 'Protective and damaging effects of stress mediators', *New England Journal of Medicine*, 338(3), 171–9.

McIntosh, P. (1988) 'White privilege and male privilege: A personal account of coming to see correspondences through work in Women's Studies', Working Paper #189, Wellesley, MA: Wellesley College Center for Research on Women02181.

McQueen, S. (2020) *Red, White and Blue*, BBC Films.

Meer, N. (2006) '"Get off your knees": Print media public intellectuals and Muslims in Britain', *Journalism Studies*, 7(1), 35–59.

Meer, N. (2008) 'The politics of voluntary and involuntary identities: are Muslims in Britain an ethnic, racial or religious minority?', *Patterns of Prejudice*, 41(5), 61–81.

Meer, N. (2010) *Citizenship, Identity and the Politics of Multiculturalism*, Basingstoke: Palgrave (1st edition).

Meer, N. (2012) 'Misrecognising Muslim consciousness in Europe', *Ethnicities*, 12(2), 178–97.

Meer, N. (2013a) 'Scales, semantics, and solidarities in the study of antisemitism and Islamophobia', *Ethnic and Racial Studies*, 36(3), pp 500–15.

Meer, N. (2013b) 'Racialization and religion: Race, culture and difference in the study of antisemitism and Islamophobia', *Ethnic and Racial Studies*, 36(3), pp 385–98.

Meer, N. (ed) (2014a) *Racialization and Religion*, Abingdon: Routledge.

Meer, N. (2014b) *Key Concepts in Race and Ethnicity*, London: SAGE.

Meer, N. (2014c) 'Islamophobia and postcolonialism: continuity, Orientalism and Muslim consciousness', *Patterns of Prejudice*, 48(5), 500–15.

Meer, N. (2015) 'Looking up in Scotland? Multinationalism, multiculturalism and political elites', *Ethnic and Racial Studies*, 38(9), 1477–96.

Meer, N. (ed) (2017) *Islam and Modernity* (Volumes 1–4), Critical Concepts in Sociology, Abingdon: Routledge.

Meer, N. (2018a) 'W.E.B. Du Bois, double consciousness and the "spirit" of recognition', *The Sociological Review*, 67(1), 47–62.

Meer, N. (2018b) 'Race and postcolonialism: Should one come before the other?', *Ethnic and Racial Studies*, 46(1), 1163–1181.

Meer, N. (2018c) 'Race Equality After Enoch Powell', *The Political Quarterly*, 89(3), 417–33.

Meer, N. (2020a) *The Edinburgh Race Lectures: After Utøya – Sifting the Wreckage of White Supremacy*, 16 September, https://www.race.ed.ac.uk/recorded-events/

Meer, N. (2020b) 'White supremacist murderers' conspiracy theories have entered mainstream European politics', *The Scotsman*, 15 September. Available at: https://www.scotsman.com/news/opinion/columnists/white-supremacist-murderers-conspiracy-theories-have-entered-mainstream-european-politics-professor-nasar-meer-2971304

Meer, N. and Modood, T. (2009) 'Refutations of racism in the "Muslim question"', *Patterns of Prejudice*, 43(3/4), 332–51.

Meer, N. and Noorani, T. (2008) 'A sociological comparison of anti-Semitism and anti-Muslim sentiment', *The Sociological Review*, 56(2), 195–219.

Meer, N. and Villegas, L. (2020) *The Impact of COVID-19 on Global Migration*, Edinburgh: University of Edinburgh.

Meer, N., Dwyer, C. and Modood, T. (2010) 'Embodying nationhood? Conceptions of British national identity, citizenship and gender in the "veil affair"', *The Sociological Review*, 58(1), 84–111.

Meer, N., Dimaio, C., Hill, E., Angeli, M., Oberg, K. and Emilsson, H. (2021) 'Governing displaced migration in Europe: housing and the role of the "local"', *Comparative Migration Studies*, 9(2), doi.org/10.1186/s40878-020-00209-x

Mercuse, H. (1968) *Negations: Essays in Critical Theory*, Boston: Beacon Press.

Mignolo, W. (2009) 'Epistemic disobedience, independent thought and de-colonial freedom', *Theory, Culture & Society*, 26(7–8): 1–23.

Miles, R. (1987) *Capitalism and Unfree Labour: Anomaly or Necessity?*, London: Tavistock.

Miles, R. (1988) 'Racism, Marxism and British politics', *Economy and Society*, 17(3): 428–60.

Miles, B. (1989) *Racism*, London: Routledge.

Mills, C. Wright (1959) *The Sociological Imagination* (40th anniversary edn), Oxford: Oxford University.

Mills, C.W. (1997) *The Racial Contract*, Ithaca: Cornell University Press.

Mills, C.W. (2007) 'White ignorance', in S. Sullivan and N. Tuana (eds), *Race and Epistemologies of Ignorance*, Albany, NY: State University of New York Press.

Mills, C.W. (2011) 'Artificial persons, natural sub-persons: Hobbes's Aristotelian contractarianism', in *Racism and Modernity, A Festschrift for Wulf D. Hund*, Berlin: LIT Verlag, pp 55–67.

Mills, C.W. (2013) 'Retrieving Rawls for racial justice? A critique of Tommie Shelby', *Critical Philosophy of Race*, 1(1), 1–27.

Mills, C.W. (2015) 'Global White ignorance', in M. Gross and L. McGoey (eds), *International Handbook of Ignorance Studies*, London: Routledge, pp 217–27.

Mills, C.W. (2018) 'Racial justice', *Aristotelian Society Supplementary*, 92(1), 69–89.

Mills, C.W. (2020) 'Theorizing racial justice', University of Michigan Tanner Lecture, https://tannerlectures.utah.edu/_resources/documents/a-to-z/m/MILLSTANNERLECTURE.pdf

Milsum, J.H. (1968) *Positive Feedback: A General Systems Approach to Positive/Negative Feedback and Mutual Causality*, London: Pergamon.

Ministry of Housing, Communities and Local Government (2018) 'UK government ethnicity facts and figures, housing, Renting Social Housing', https://www.ethnicity-facts-figures.service.gov.uk/housing/social-housing/renting-from-a-local-authority-or-housing-association-social-housing/1.3

Minow, M. (1997) *Not Only for Myself: Identity, Politics and the Law*, New York: The New York Press.

Mitchell, T. (1991) 'The limits of the state: Beyond statist approaches and their critics', *American Political Science Review*, 85, 77–96.

Modood, T. (1992) *Not Easy Being British: Culture, Colour and Citizenship*, London: Trentham Books.

Modood, T. (2005) *Multicultural Politics: Racism, Ethnicity and Muslims in Britain*, Edinburgh: Edinburgh University Press.

Mohammed, A.O., Attalla, B., Bashir, F.M., Ahmed, F.E., El Hassan, A.M., Ibnauf, G., Jiang, W., Cavalli-Sforza, L.L., Karrar, Z.A. and Ibrahim, M.E. (2006) 'Relationship of the sickle cell gene to the ethnic and geographic groups populating the Sudan', *Community Genetics*, 9(2), 113–20.

Mohdin, A. (2021) 'Experts cited in No 10's race report claim they were not properly consulted', *The Guardian*, https://www.theguardian.com/world/2021/apr/01/experts-cited-in-no-10s-race-report-claim-they-were-not-properly-consulted

Mondon, A. and Winter, A. (2020) *Reactionary Democracy: How Racism and the Populist Far Right Became Mainstream*, New York: Verso Books.

Moses, A.D. (2002) 'Conceptual blockages and definitional dilemmas in the "racial century": genocides of indigenous peoples and the Holocaust', *Patterns of Prejudice*, 36(4), 7–36.

Mosse, G.L. (1995) 'Racism and nationalism', *Nations and Nationalism*, 1(2), 163–73.

Muir, H., Shaheen, F., Andrews, K., and Foster, D. (2017) 'May's race disparity audit – our panellists give their verdict', *The Guardian*, 10 October, https://www.theguardian.com/commentisfree/2017/oct/10/theresa-may-race-audit-guardian-panel

Myrberg, G. (2017) 'Local challenges and national concerns: municipal level responses to national refugee settlement policies in Denmark and Sweden', *International Review of Administrative Sciences*, 83(2), 322–39.

Nagpaul, C. (2020) 'The disproportionate impact of COVID-19 on ethnic minority healthcare workers', *BMJ* blog, 20 April, https://blogs.bmj.com/bmj/2020/04/20/chaandnagpaul-the-disproportionate-impact-of-COVID-19-onethnic-minority-healthcare-workers/

NAO (National Audit Office) (2018) *Handling of the Windrush situation*, 5 December, https://www.nao.org.uk/report/handling-of-the-windrush-situation/

Nazroo, J. (1998) 'Rethinking the relationship between ethnicity and mental health: the British Fourth National Survey of Ethnic Minorities', *Social Psychiatry and Psychiatric Epidemiology*, 33(4), 145–8.

Nguyen, L.H. et al (2020) 'Risk of COVID-19 among front-line health-care workers and the general community: a prospective cohort study', *The Lancet Public Health*, 5(9), e475–e483.

O'Leary, B. (2006) 'Liberalism, multiculturalism, Danish cartoons, Islamist fraud, and the rights of the ungodly', *International Migration*, 44(5): 22–33.

Olsen, A.L., Kyhse-Andersen, J.H. and Moynihan, D. (2020) 'The unequal distribution of opportunity: a national audit study of bureaucratic discrimination in primary school access', *American Journal of Political Science*, https://doi.org/10.1111/ajps.12584

Olusoga, D. (2018) 'The Treasury's tweet shows slavery is still misunderstood', *The Guardian*, 12 February, https://www.theguardian.com/commentisfree/2018/feb/12/treasury-tweet-slavery-compensate-slave-owners

Omi, M. and Winant, H. (1986) *Racial Formation in the United States*, New York: Routledge & Kegan Paul.

Omi, M. and Winant, H. (2009) 'Thinking through race and racism', *Contemporary Sociology*, 38(2), 121–5.

ONS (Office for National Statistics) (2021) 'UK government ethnicity facts and figures, unemployment', https://www.ethnicity-facts-figures.service.gov.uk/work-pay-and-benefits/unemployment-and-economic-inactivity/unemployment/latest

Orwell, G. (1949) *Nineteen Eighty-Four*, London: Martin Secker & Warburg.

Otu, A., Ahinkorah, B.O., Ameyaw, E.K., Seidu, A.A. and Yaya, S. (2020) 'One country, two crises: What COVID-19 reveals about health inequalities among ethnic minority communities in the United Kingdom and the sustainability of its health system?', *International Journal for Equity in Health*, 19(1), 1–6.

Palmer, A. (1998) 'Colonial and modern genocide: Explanations and categories', *Ethnic and Racial Studies*, 21(1), 89–115.

Palmer, A. (2000) *Colonial Genocide*, Adelaide: Crawford House.

Park, R. (1950) *Race and Culture*, Glencoe, IL: Free Press.

Parekh, B. (2000) *Rethinking Multiculturalism: Cultural Diversity and Political Theory*, Basingstoke: Palgrave.

Parekh, B. (2005) 'Redistribution or recognition? A misguided debate', in G. Loury, T. Modood and S. Teles (eds), *Ethnicity, Social Mobility and Public Policy in the US and UK*, Cambridge: Cambridge University Press.

Patterson, S. (1965) *Dark Strangers: A Sociological Study of the Absorption of a Recent West Indian Migrant Group in Brixton, South London*, London: Tavistock.

Patterson, S. (1969) *Immigration and Race Relations in Britain, 1960–1967*, London: Oxford University Press.

Pavel, T.G. (1986) *Fictional Worlds*, Boston: Harvard University Press.

PHE (Public Health England) (2020) 'Beyond the data: Understanding the impact of COVID-19 on BAME communities', https://assets.publishing.service.gov.uk/government/uploads/system/uploads/attachment_data/file/892376/COVID_stakeholder_engagement_synthesis_beyond_the_data.pdf

Phelan, J.C. and Link, B.G. (2015) 'Is racism a fundamental cause of inequalities in health?', *Annual Review of Sociology*, 41, 311–30.

Phillips, D. (2006) 'Moving towards integration: The housing of asylum seekers and refugees in Britain', *Journal of Housing Studies*, 21(4), 539–53.

Platt, O., Brambilla, D., Rosse, W., Milner, P., Castro, O., Steinberg, M. and Klug, P. (1994) 'Mortality in sickle cell disease: Life expectancy and risk factors for early death', *New England Journal of Medicine*, 330(23), 1639–44.

Powell, E. (1968) 'Rivers of blood' speech, available at: TOQ V1N1.pmd (toqonline.com)

Preston, J. and Chadderton, C. (2012) 'Rediscovering "race traitor": towards a Critical Race Theory informed public pedagogy', *Race, Ethnicity and Education*, 15(1), 85–100.

Quijano, A. (2000) 'Coloniality of power, Eurocentrism, and Latin America', *Nepantla: Views from South*, 1(3), 533–81.

Qureshi, K. (2019) *Chronic Illness in a Pakistani Labour Diaspora*, Durham: Carolina Academic Press.

Qureshi, K., Salway, S., Chowbey, P. and Platt, L. (2014) 'Long-term ill health and the social embeddedness of work: A study in a post-industrial, multi-ethnic locality in the UK', *Sociology of Health & Illness*, 36(7), 955–69.

Qureshi, K., Meer, N. and Hill, S. (2020) 'Different but similar? BAME groups and the impacts of COVID-19 in Scotland', in N. Meer, S. Akhtar and N. Davidson (eds), *Taking Stock: Race Equality in Scotland*, London: Runnymede Trust, https://www.race.ed.ac.uk/taking-stock-race-equality-in-scotland/

Rawls, J. (1999 [1971]) *A Theory of Justice*, rev. edn, Cambridge, MA: Harvard University Press.

Ray, V. (2019) 'A theory of racialized organizations', *American Sociological Review*, 84(1), 26–53.

Reay, D. (2018) 'Race and elite universities in the UK', in J. Arday and H.S. Mirza (eds), *Dismantling Race in Higher Education*, pp 47–66.

Reichenbach, H. (1976) *Modalities and Counterfactuals*, Oxford: Oxford University Press.

Rex, J. (1973) *Race, Colonialism and the City*, London: Routledge and Kegan Paul.

Rex, J. and Moore, R. (1979 [1967]) *Race, Community and Conflict: A Study of Sparkbrook*, Oxford: Oxford University Press.

Rollock, N. (2019) *Staying Power: The Career Experiences and Strategies of UK Black Female Professors*, London: UCU.

Rose, E.J.B. (1969) *Colour and Citizenship*, London: Institute for Race Relations.

Rothchild, N. (2020) 'The hidden flaw in Sweden's anti-lockdown strategy', *Foreign Policy*, https://foreignpolicy.com/2020/04/21/sweden-coronavirus-anti-lockdown-immigrants/

Rudiger, A. (2007) 'Cultures of equality, traditions of belonging', in C. Bertossi (ed), *European Anti-discrimination and the Politics of Citizenship*, Basingstoke: Palgrave Macmillan.

Salvage Editorial Collective (2020) 'The Covid state: Dispatch three from a changing world', https://salvage.zone/articles/the-covid-state-dispatch-three-from-a-changing-world/

Salway, S. et al (2020) 'Transforming the health system for the UK's multiethnic population', *BMJ*, 368, m268.

Sassen, S. (1991) *The Global City*. Princeton, NJ: Princeton University Press.

Savoca, M.R., Quandt, S.A., Evans, C.D., Flint, T.L., Bradfield, A.G., Morton, T.B., Harshfield, G.A. and Ludwig, D.A. (2009) 'Views of hypertension among young African Americans who vary in their risk of developing hypertension', *Ethnicity & Disease*, 19(1), 28–34.

Scarman Report (1981) *The Brixton Disorders 10–12 April 1981: Report of an Inquiry by the Rt. Hon. The Lord Scarman, OBE*, Cmnd 8247, London: HMSO.

Schwarz, B. (1986) 'Conservatism, nationalism and imperialism', in J. Donald and S. Hall (eds), *Politics and Ideology*, Milton Keynes: Open University Press.

Scott, J. (1999) *The Conundrum of Equality*, Paper Number 2, School of Social Sciences, Institute for Advanced Study, Princeton University.

Scottish Diabetes Data Group (2018) *Scottish Diabetes Survey*, https://www.diabetesinscotland.org.uk/wpcontent/uploads/2019/12/Scottish-Diabetes-Survey2018.pdf

Seamster, L. and Ray, V. (2018) 'Against teleology in the study of race: Toward the abolition of the progress paradigm', *Sociological Theory*, 36(4), 315–42.

Seeley, J.R. (1971 [1883]) *The Expansion of England*, Chicago: The University of Chicago Press.

Sewell, T. (2009) *Generating Genius: Black Boys in Love, Ritual and Schooling*. Stoke: Trentham.

Sewell, A. (2016) 'The racism–race reification process: A meso-level political economic framework for understanding racial health disparities', *Sociology of Race and Ethnicity*, 2(4), 402–32.

Shapiro, J. (1996) *Shakespeare and the Jews*, New York: Columbia University Press.

Shapiro, J. (2000) *Oberammergau: The Troubling Story of the World's Most Famous Passion Play*, New York: Pantheon Books.

Sharply, M.S. (2001) 'Understanding the excess of psychosis among the African-Caribbean population in England – review of current hypotheses', *British Journal of Psychiatry*, 178(40): 60–8.

Shields, A., Faustini, S.E., Perez-Toledo, M., Jossi, S., Aldera, E., Allen, J.D. and Richter, A.G. (2020) 'SARS-CoV-2 seroprevalence and asymptomatic viral carriage in healthcare workers: a cross-sectional study', *Thorax*, 75(12), 1089–94.

Shulman, G. (2011) 'Acknowledgment and disavowal as an idiom for theorizing politics', *Theory & Event*, 14(1), doi: 10.1353/tae.2011.000

Sicakkan, G.H. and Lithman, Y. (2005) 'Politics of identity: Modes of belonging and citizenship: An overview of conceptual and theoretical challenges', in G.H. Sicakkan and Y. Lithman (eds), *Changing the Basis of Citizenship in the Modern State*, Lampeter: The Edwin Mellen Press.

Siddique, H. (2020) 'UK Government urged to investigate coronavirus deaths of BAME doctors', *The Guardian*, 10 April, https://www.theguardian.com/society/2020/apr/10/ukcoronavirus-deaths-bame-doctors-bma

Sirleaf, M. (2021) 'Disposable lives: COVID-19, vaccines, and the uprising', *Faculty Scholarship*, 1648, https://digitalcommons.law.umaryland.edu/fac_pubs/1648

Sky News (2011) 'The faces of Norway massacre victims', 27 July.

Smith, A.D. (2009) *Ethnosymbolism and Nationalism. A Cultural Approach*, London: Routledge.

Smith, D.J. (1976) *The Facts of Racial Disadvantage*, London: Political and Economic Planning.

Smith, K. (2010) 'Research, policy and funding: academic treadmills and the squeeze on intellectual spaces', *The British Journal of Sociology*, 61(1), 176–95.

Smith W.A., Allen, W.R. and Danley, L.L. (2007) '"Assume the position … you fit the description": Psychosocial experiences and racial battle fatigue among African American male college students', *American Behavioral Scientist*, 51(4), 551–78, doi:10.1177/0002764207307742

Solomos, J. (1993) *Race and Racism in Britain*, Basingstoke: Macmillan.

Solomos, J. and Back, L. (1994) 'Conceptualizing racisms: Social theory, politics and research', *Sociology*, 28(1), 143–61.

Specia, M. (2019) 'The New Zealand shooting victims spanned generations and nationalities', *The New York Times*, 19 March, https://www.nytimes.com/2019/03/19/world/asia/new-zealand-shooting-victims-names.html

Steel, D. (1968) *No Entry*, London: Hurst.

Steiner, G. (1961) *The Death of Tragedy*, New Haven, CT: Yale University Press.

Steyn, M. (2006a) *America Alone: The End of the World As We Know It*, New York: Regnery Publishing.

Steyn, M. (2006b) 'European population will be "40 percent Muslim" by 2025', *Wall Street Journal*, 4 January.

Stoler, A.L. (1995) *Race and the Education of Desire: Foucault's History of Sexuality and the Colonial Order of Things*, London: Duke University Press.

Stone, D. (2018) 'Refugees then and now: memory, history and politics in the long twentieth century: an introduction', *Patterns of Prejudice*, 52(2–3), 101–6, doi: 10.1080/0031322X.2018.1433004

Syal, R. (2021) 'Doreen Lawrence says No 10 report gives "racists the green light"', https://www.theguardian.com/world/2021/apr/01/doreen-lawrence-says-no-10-report-gives-racists-the-green-light

Thomas, J.M. (2010) 'The racial formation of Medieval Jews: A challenge to the field', *Ethnic and Racial Studies*, 33(10), 1737–55.

Tondo, L. (2020) 'Matteo Salvini goes on trial over migrant kidnapping charges', *The Guardian*, 2 October, https://www.theguardian.com/world/2020/oct/02/matteo-salvini-set-to-be-tried-over-migrant-kidnapping-charges-italy

Trilling, D. (2020) 'Migrants aren't spreading coronavirus – but nationalists are blaming them anyway', *The Guardian*, 28 February, https://www.theguardian.com/commentisfree/2020/feb/28/coronavirus-outbreak-migrants-blamed-italy-matteo-salvini-marine-le-pen

TUC (Trades Union Congress) (2012) 'Youth unemployment and ethnicity', https://www.tuc.org.uk/sites/default/files/BMEyouthunemployment.pdf

TUC (2019) 'BME workers far more likely to be trapped in insecure work, TUC analysis reveals', 12 April, https://www.tuc.org.uk/news/bme-workers-far-more-likely-be-trapped-insecure-work-tuc-analysis-reveals

Tudor, A. (2018) 'Cross-fadings of racialisation and migratisation: The postcolonial turn in Western European gender and migration studies', *Gender, Place & Culture*, 25(7), 1057–72.

Twine, F. and Gallagher, C. (2008) 'The future of whiteness: a map of the "third wave"', *Ethnic and Racial Studies*, 31(1): 4–24.

Uberoi, V. (2015) 'The "Parekh Report": National identities without nations and nationalism', *Ethnicities*, 15(4), 509–26.

Uberoi, V. and Modood, T. (2013) 'Inclusive Britishness: A multiculturalist advance', *Political Studies* 61(1), 23–41.

UK Government (2018) 'Ethnicity facts and figures: employment by sector', 10 October, https://www.ethnicity-facts-figures.service.gov.uk/work-pay-and-benefits/employment/employment-by-sector/latest#by-ethnicity-and-sector

UK Government (2021) Response to the Committee's Eleventh Report of Session 2019–21, Fourth Special Report, 5 February 2021.

UNHCR (United Nations High Commissioner for Refugees) (1951) The 1951 Convention Relating to the Status of Refugees, UNHCR. Available at: https://www.unhcr.org/4ca34be29.pdf

UNHCR (2020a) 'UNHCR UK FAQs on COVID-19 in relation to refugees and asylum seekers', https://www.unhcr.org/uk/unhcr-uk-faqs-on-covid-19-in-relation-to-refugees-and-asylum-seekers.html

UNHCR (2020b) 'UNHCR UK statement on the situation at the Turkey–EU Border', https://www.unhcr.org/uk/news/press/2020/3/5e5d08ad4/unhcr-statement-situation-turkey-eu-border.html

Valluvan, S. (2017) 'Defining and challenging new nationalism', *The Sociological Review*, https://thesociologicalreview.org/collections/sociology-of-brexit/defining-and-challenging-new-nationalism/

Vandevoordt, R. (2019) 'The European refugee controversy: Civil solidarity, cultural imaginaries and political change', *Social Inclusion*, 7(2), 48–52.

Venn, C. (2003) *The Postcolonial Challenge: Towards Alternative Worlds*, London: SAGE.

Vernon, P. (2020) 'Paulette Wilson remembered by Patrick Vernon', *The Guardian*, 20 December, https://www.theguardian.com/world/2020/dec/14/paulette-wilson-remembered-by-patrick-vernon

Vickerman, S. (2013) *The Problem of Post-Racialism*, Basingstoke: Palgrave, p 8.

Virdee, S. (2014) *Racism, Class and the Racialized Outsider*, London: Macmillan International Higher Education.

Von Bertalanffy, L. (1968) *General System Theory: Foundations, Development, Application*, New York: George Braziller.

Von Bertalanffy (1972) 'The history and status of general systems theory', in G.J. Klir (ed), *Trends in General Systems Theory*, New York: John Wiley & Sons, Inc.

Wachsmuth, D. (2012) 'Three ecologies: urban metabolism and the society–nature opposition', *The Sociological Quarterly*, 53(4), 506–23.

Wacquant, L.J.D. (1998) 'Negative social capital: State breakdown and social destitution in America's urban core', *The Netherlands Journal of the Built Environment*, 13(1), 25–40.

Wang, J. (2018) *Carceral Capitalism*, South Pasadena, CA: Semiotext(e).

Washington, H.A. (2007) *Medical Apartheid: The Dark History of Medical Experimentation on Black Americans from Colonial Times to the Present*, New York: Doubleday Books.

Weber, M. (1922) 'The city (non-legitimate domination)', in G. Roth and C. Wittich (eds), *Economy and Society: An Outline of Interpretive Sociology*, trs. E. Fischoff et al, Berkeley, CA: University of California Press, 2 vols, Vol 2, ch XVI, pp 1212–372.

Wekker, G. (2016) *White Innocence: Paradoxes of Colonialism and Race*, Durham, NC: Duke University Press.

West, C. (1989) *The American Evasion of Philosophy: A Genealogy of Pragmatism*, Madison, WI: University of Wisconsin.

Williams, E. (1944) *Capitalism and Slavery*, Chapel Hill, NC: University of North Carolina Press.

Williams, M. (2003) 'Citizenship as identity, citizenship as shared fate, and the functions of multicultural education', in K. McDonough and W. Feinberg (eds), *Citizenship and Education in Liberal-Democratic Societies: Teaching for Cosmopolitan Values and Collective Identities*, Oxford: Oxford University Press.

Williams, W. (2020) *Windrush Lessons Learned Review: Independent review by Wendy Williams*, London: HMSO.

Williams, D.R. and Mohammed, S.A. (2013) 'Racism and health I: Pathways and scientific evidence', *American Behavioural Scientist*, 57(8), 1152–73.

Winant, H. (2001a) 'The making and unmaking of whiteness', in B.B. Rasmussen, E. Klinenberg, I.J. Nexica and M. Wray (eds), *The Making and Unmaking of Whiteness*, Durham, NC and London: Duke University Press.

Winant, H. (2001b) *The World is a Ghetto: Race and Democracy Since World War II*, New York: Basic Books.

Wolfe, P. (2016) *Traces of History: Elementary Structures of Race*, London: Verso.

Wood, V. (2020) 'Teachers presenting white privilege as fact are breaking the law, minister warns', *The Independent*, https://www.independent.co.uk/news/uk/politics/kemi-badenoch-black-history-month-white-privilege-black-lives-matter-b1189547.html

Wood, M., Hales, J., Purdon, S. et al (2009) *A test for racial discrimination in recruitment practice in British cities*, Research report 607, London: Department for Work and Pensions.

Young, I.M. (1990) *Justice and the Politics of Difference*, Princeton, NJ: Princeton University Press.

Young, I.M. (1995) 'Polity and group difference: a critique of the ideal of the universal citizenship', in R. Beiner (ed), *Theorising Citizenship*, Albany, NY: State University of New York Press.

Younis, J. (2020) 'BAME doctors like me are expected to put up and shut up – I fear that's the real reason we're dying'. *The Independent*, 20 April https://www.independent.co.uk/voices/coronavirus-nhsdoctors-nurses-ppe-bame-deaths-discriminationa9473741.html

Youth Justice Statistics (2018/19) England and Wales, Youth Justice Board/Ministry of Justice, youth-justice-statistics-bulletin-march-2019.pdf (publishing.service.gov.uk)

Yuval-Davis, N., Wemyss, G. and Cassidy, K. (2018) 'Everyday bordering, belonging and the reorientation of British immigration legislation', *Sociology*, 52(2), 228–44.

Zerka, P. (2020) 'Ill will: populism and the coronavirus', https://ecfr.eu/article/commentary_ill_will_populism_and_the_coronavirus/

Zubaida, S. (1972) 'Sociologists and race relations', in J. Floud, P. Lewis and R. Stuart (eds), *Problems and Prospects of Socio-legal Research: Proceedings of a Seminar*, Oxford: Nuffield College.

Zwysen, W., Di Stasio, V. and Heath, A. (2020) 'Ethnic penalties and hiring discrimination: comparing results from observational studies with field experiments in the UK', *Sociology*, https://doi.org/10.1177/0038038520966947

Index